BOURNEMOUTH'S
FOUNDERS AND
FAMOUS VISITORS

BOURNEMOUTH'S
FOUNDERS AND
FAMOUS VISITORS

ANDREW NORMAN

First published 2010

The History Press
The Mill, Brimscombe Port
Stroud, Gloucestershire, GL5 2QG
www.thehistorypress.co.uk

ISBN 978 0 7524 5088 9

Typesetting and origination by The History Press
Printed in India by Aegean Offset Printers, New Delhi

Contents

	Acknowledgments	6
	About the Author	7
	Preface	8
1.	Sir George Ivison Tapps (1st Baronet)	11
2.	Lewis and Henrietta Tregonwell	14
3.	Sir George William Tapps Gervis (2nd Baronet)	23
4.	Benjamin Ferrey	26
5.	Sir George Eliott Meyrick Tapps Gervis Meyrick (3rd Baronet)	31
6.	Decimus Burton	32
7.	Dr Augustus Bozzi Granville	35
8.	The Reverend Alexander Morden Bennett	38
9.	Georgina and Mary Talbot	44
10.	Sir Percy and Lady Shelley	47
11.	Christopher Crabbe Creeke	51
12.	Charles Lavington Pannel	56
13.	W.H. Smith and Family	62
14.	Others associated with the National Sanatorium	69
15.	Sir Henry and Lady Taylor	72
16.	Charles Darwin	74
17.	Lucy Kemp-Welch	76
18.	The Reverend John Keble	82
19.	Thomas and Emma Hardy	84
20.	Sir Merton and Lady Russell-Cotes	86
21.	Lillie Langtry	93
22.	Dr Horace Dobell and his wife Elizabeth	100
23.	Robert Louis and Fanny Stevenson	107
24.	Frederick W. Lacey	115
25.	Sir Winston Churchill	121
26.	Guglielmo Marconi	123
27.	Flora Thompson	128
28.	D.H. Lawrence	133
29.	J.R.R. Tolkien	137
	Appendix	145
	Epilogue	147
	Bibliography	153
	Index	155

Acknowledgments

The British Medical Association; Bournemouth Borough Council; *Daily Echo*, Bournemouth; East Dorset NHS Library Service; Court Royal, Bournemouth; The Forestry Commission; Harrow School Archive; Hastings Museum & Art Gallery; The Heritage Zone, Bournemouth Library; Hotel Miramar; The Keep Military Museum, Dorchester; Langtry Manor; The Meyrick Estate; Museum of the Royal Pharmaceutical Society of Great Britain; The New Forest Museum; RIBA Library Photograph Collection; The Robert Louis Stevenson Club; Royal College of Physicians of London; The Royal Library, Windsor Castle; Royal London Archives and Museum; Rural Life Centre, Tilford, Surrey; Ryde Social Heritage Group; Russell-Cotes Art Gallery & Museum.

Michael Andrews; Fraser Donachie; Hilary Ferrey-Groves; John Gill; Janette Gregson; David Harrison; Scott Harrison; Kate Heard; Dr Arthur T. Hendry; Miles Howard; Pamela Howard; Peter Kazmierczak; Tim Malpas; Stephen Malton; Alan Marchbank; Jan Marsh; Hugh Milner; Brenda B. Morgan; Harry Oram; Richard Reeves; Kate Richardson; Chris Shepheard; Nick Speakman; Duncan Walker; and Chris Wheeler.

I am grateful to Mrs Julia E. Smith of Edmonsham House, a descendant of Lewis Tregonwell, and to Sir George Meyrick (7th Baronet, and descendant of Sir George Ivison Tapps, 1st Baronet).

I am deeply grateful to my beloved wife Rachel, for all her help and encouragement.

About the Author

Andrew Norman was born in Newbury, Berkshire, UK, in 1943. Having been educated at Thornhill High School, Gwelo, Southern Rhodesia (now Zimbabwe) and St Edmund Hall, Oxford, he qualified in medicine at the Radcliffe Infirmary. He has two children, Bridget and Thomas, by his first wife.

From 1972-83, Andrew worked as a general practitioner in Poole, Dorset, before a spinal injury cut short his medical career. He is now an established writer whose published works include biographies of Thomas Hardy, T.E. Lawrence, Sir Francis Drake, Adolf Hitler, Robert Mugabe, Agatha Christie, Enid Blyton, Jane Austen and Sir Arthur Conan Doyle. Andrew was remarried to Rachel in 2005.

Andrew Norman's books are displayed on his website: andrew-norman.com.

Preface

If it were possible for a resident of modern-day Bournemouth to travel backwards in time to the early 1800s, such a person might be surprised at the sight which met their eyes. Here was a wild and virtually uninhabited heathland, bisected by picturesque valleys called 'chines', by rough roads used by travellers by day, and, allegedly, by smugglers by night, and by trackways made by the red, fallow, and roe deer, which were indigenous to the area. Here were to be found less than a handful of dwellings, including an inn, frequented by travellers, and a decoy house, designed to accommodate the Lord of the Manor and his friends when they came to shoot duck on the adjacent decoy pond. How did Bournemouth evolve from this into a bustling modern town, all in the space of two centuries? And who were the people responsible for its remarkable evolution?

Since the Middle Ages, the land of England had been divided into parcels – manors – each one owned and presided over by its feudal lord. However, whereas the lord owned the manor, ordinary people – 'commoners' – had certain traditional rights in regard to those portions of 'common land' which were included in it, as will shortly be seen.

The land on which central Bournemouth now stands was situated at the south side of the Tithing (rural division) of Holdenhurst which, in turn, was part of the Liberty of Westover – a Liberty being a region where the owner was entitled to certain rights, by virtue of his possession of it.

In 1708, Sir Peter Mews of Hinton Admiral in Hampshire, became Lord of the Liberty of Westover and of the adjacent Manor of Christchurch. When he married, he settled both estates on his wife, Lydia. When Lydia died without issue in 1751, the manor passed to her nephew Benjamin Clerke, son of her sister Agnes, and thence, on Benjamin's death in 1758, to Benjamin's son, Joseph Jarvis Clerke, who died in 1777, also without issue. The manor then passed to Joseph's cousin, Sir George Ivison Tapps, who is chosen to be the first character mentioned in this volume.

The *Concise Oxford Dictionary of English Place-names* reveals that in the fifteenth and sixteenth centuries, the place where the Bourne stream met the sea was called 'La Bournemowthe'. However, the date of the founding of Bournemouth is usually taken as the year 1810, which was when a parcel of land was conveyed by Sir George Ivison Tapps to Lewis Dymoke Grosvenor Tregonwell, on which the latter proposed to build a house.

A measure of just how remote and isolated the region that became Bournemouth was, is indicated in a survey made by Lord Thomas Poulet, Earl of Southampton, and others in June 1574:

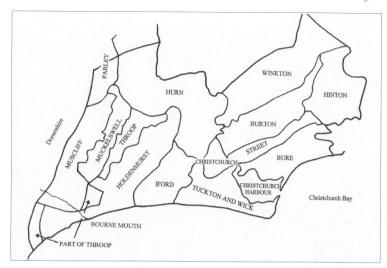

The Liberty of
Westover.

First, wee finde at Bourne mouth: within the west baye at Christchurche a place very easy for
the ennemye to lande there conteyning by estimacion oon quarter of a myle in length, being
voyde of all inhabiting.[1]

In other words, no one lived in the vicinity. Who the potential enemy was is not specified,
but the most likely contenders would appear to be Spain – whose Armada was subsequently
defeated in 1588 – and France.

By 1805, when the Duke of Rutland published his *Journal of a Tour around the Southern
Coasts of England*, little had changed:

From Christchurch, we proceeded on horseback towards Poole… on the barren, uncultivated
heath where we were, there was not a human being to direct us.[2]

In the same year, 1805, antiquarian and topographer Edward Wedlake Brayley went further,
describing the region (in a somewhat unflattering way) as a, 'most dreary waste,' whose only
function was, 'to supply the neighbouring villages with firing' (by which he meant turf,
which was dug for use as fuel). Henrietta Tregonwell, wife of the aforementioned Lewis,
did not share this view, thus proving truth of the old adage – that beauty is in the eye of
the beholder. When she arrived here, she was captivated by its wild and untamed beauty;
so much so that she decided that this is where she would like to have a summer residence.

What better way to celebrate the bicentenary of the founding of modern-day
Bournemouth, therefore, than to write an account of a selection of those people – both
resident and non-resident – who were instrumental either in transforming the wild heathland
at the mouth of the Bourne into a settlement which eventually became a town, or who
subsequently came here as would-be residents or visitors, to add life and drama to the place?

'Bourne' referred to the area in the vicinity of the Bourne, the rivulet which ran through
the Bourne Chine (a 'chine' being a steep-sided valley where a river or stream flows
through seaside cliffs and into the sea; the name deriving from the Old English word 'cinu'

– a cleft or chink). 'Bourne Mouth' referred to the lower end of Bourne Chine, where the Bourne met the sea. The catalyst for the development of 'Bourne' was the passing, between 1760 and 1820 of the Enclosure Acts, which decreed that the common land which had traditionally been available to ordinary people for the purposes of pasturing their animals and collecting fuel, was to be sold off.

Commissioners Richard Richardson of Lincoln's Inn Fields, John Wickens of Mapperton, Dorset, and William Clapcott of Holdenhurst were made responsible for the Christchurch Enclosure Award (completed in 1805, following the Christchurch Enclosure Act of 1802), by which the land was divided into lots and sold. The Commissioners were also responsible for creating, 'Roads, Bridle Ways and Footways' across the large expanse of heathland. Prior to this there were only sandy trackways – perhaps wide enough to accommodate a smuggler's horse and cart – leading eastward to Pokesdown, Iford, Christchurch, and Mudeford; northward to Kinson and Throop; north-eastward to Holdenhurst, and westward to Poole.

The outcome was that the enclosed land was now purchased, principally by seven persons, as listed below: [3]

		Acres
William Dean	West Cliff, King's Park	500
William Driver	Redhill, Meyrick Park	236
Sir George I. Tapps	South and East Cliffs	205
Philip Norris	Boscombe, Strouden	152
Cornelius Trim	Charminster	82
Lord Malmesbury	Iford, Moordown, Strouden	59
Arthur Quartley	Near Stokewood Road	21

Another 127 persons also acquired land under the terms of the Enclosure Award.

Tapps himself purchased additional tracts of land on the East Cliff and at Southbourne, so that the entire seafront between Boscombe and Bournemouth (excluding Boscombe Chine) came into his possession. However, five plots of land, totalling 425 acres and held in trust by Tapps, were set aside where the commoners could continue to obtain their supplies of turf and timber for fuel.

It was Lewis Tregonwell who, in the summer of 1810, came to 'Bourne' with his wife Henrietta, and proceeded to build a house there (which was not, contrary to popular belief, the first house to be built at Bourne, as will shortly be seen), together with a handful of cottages, some of which were let to visitors. Bournemouth, however, in its early years, did not evolve primarily as a retirement or tourist resort. The town's motto is *Pulchritudo et Salubritas* – 'Beauty and Health', reflecting the fact that Bournemouth originally developed, in the main, as a health resort.

It was Dr Augustus B. Granville who popularized Bournemouth by including it in his guidebook entitled *The Spas of England*, published in 1841. He also suggested ways in which the town might be improved and beautified. Thereafter, the town became a magnet for those seeking treatment from the many medical experts who resided there. Others visited Bournemouth, or chose to reside there, for reasons other than their health.

Of the noteworthy personalities selected for this volume, each has a unique story to tell, and, as will be seen, Bournemouth is an altogether more colourful and interesting place because of their association with it.

1

Sir George Ivison Tapps (1st Baronet)

Sir George Ivison Tapps, born on 5 January 1753, was the son of George Gervis Tapps, barrister of Hinton Admiral, Hampshire. In 1778, Tapps inherited the Manors of Christchurch and Hinton Admiral, together with the Liberty of Westover (formerly the estates of Sir Peter Mews) from his cousin, Joseph Jarvis Clerke. This included the Mews family mansion at Hinton Admiral. On 29 July 1790, Tapps married Sarah, daughter of Barrington Buggin, merchant of London and on 28 July 1791, he was created baronet.

Tapps, as Lord of the Manor, played a leading part in the implementation of the Christchurch Enclosure Award of 1805, which was concerned with the enclosure, distribution, and sale of the common land. The 200 acres of the East Cliff, together with 'six large pieces' of land on the south side of Christchurch, Old Christchurch and Commercial Roads, and several other plots elsewhere (which he purchased from the Enclosure Commissioners) represented, in the words of historian Charles H. Mate, 'the very pick of Bournemouth.'[1]

On his newly-acquired swathes of heathland situated in the vicinity of the Bourne, Tapps proceeded to plant Scots Pines; an event of some significance, because, as will be seen, the pine tree was of great importance to the development of Bournemouth. This is reflected in the fact that a pine tree features prominently on Bournemouth's coat of arms. Tapps was also instrumental in promoting the Christian religion in the area, donating the land at nearby Holdenhurst on which the new Church of St John the Evangelist was built and which opened in 1834.

Tapps undoubtedly appreciated that the land which he had acquired – especially that situated near to the sea front – was of great potential value for property development. However, to his credit, he also had an eye for a beautiful landscape. With the aid of London architect and garden designer Decimus Burton (q.v.), he had already planted 150,000 trees on his estate in the East End of London. Tapps now proceeded, on his newly-acquired estates at Bourne, to replace the 'heather, gorse, and sandy waste' with plantations of pine trees.[2]

The Scots Pine (*pinus sylvestris*) is indigenous to Britain. However, by the seventeenth century the species had virtually disappeared from England and Wales as a result of an excessive demand for timber, and of the deliberate clearance of land. In fact, an early map of the Bournemouth area dated 1805-07, and the Ordnance Survey map dated 1809-11, show no significant woods or plantations of trees whatsoever within a 2½-mile radius of 'Bourne Mouth'. Remarkably, within little over half a century, all this was to change, and Philip Brannon's map from around 1860, reveals great swathes of woodland and plantations, notably to the east of Bournemouth, between it and Boscombe (Hinton Wood), to the west of the town (Bourne Valley), to the north (Talbot Woods), and to the north-east (Springbourne/Queen's Park).

Scots Pines, however, were susceptible to drought, and they were therefore gradually replaced by the more hardy Maritime Pine (*pinus pinaster*), which was introduced to southern Hampshire from the Landes region of south-west France in 1805. Other varieties grown included the Austrian, Weymouth, and Monterey Pines.

It is not suggested that Tapps was the first person to plant pine trees in the area. For example, author Felicity A. Woodhead points out that four 'Scots firs' were planted at Heron Court, Holdenhurst, seat of the Earls of Malmesbury, as early as 1746. However, Tapps does appear to have been the first to plant them in the vicinity of Bourne. His neighbours subsequently followed suit.

Did any dwelling places exist in the immediate vicinity of the Bourne in the days of Sir George Tapps? The answer, surprisingly, is yes. A document of sale, dated 25 September 1810, and referring to land which is in the very heart of modern-day Bournemouth, refers to a, 'footpath or way leading from the decoy and cottage by the decoy enclosures…'.[3] Such 'enclosures' were probably for the huntsmen to hide behind as they went about their business of shooting ducks on the nearby decoy pond. However, the only dwelling shown on maps of the area is 'Bourne House', situated adjacent to and to the west of the Bourne, and about ½ a mile from the lower end of Bourne Chine. For example, 'Bourne House' is depicted on Isaac Taylor's map of 1759, on Thomas Milne's map of 1791, and on John Cary's map (as 'Bourn House') of 1804. The conclusion must be, therefore, that 'Bourne House' and the decoy house are one and the same, and that the property was situated approximately where the modern-day 'Square' is today (the inappropriately named Square being at the centre of the town, where the Christchurch, Wimborne and Poole Roads met, and where, in 1849, a bridge was built across the Bourne). The location of the decoy pond is not indicated on either map, but doubtless it was situated near to the decoy house (perhaps where the Upper Pleasure Gardens are situated today).

It may be assumed, therefore, that Bourne House was the abode of the decoy man (who was employed in decoying wild fowl). It is likely that it was a substantial property, which could also house those of the shooting party who came to visit – presumably at the invitation of the Lord of the Manor.

According to the Malmesbury Estate Tithe Survey of 1796, the grounds of Bourne House comprised seven acres in all, and included a house-garden, seven meadows and a bee garden. The image of the decoy man, tending to bees, which in turn gathered nectar from heathers which grew in profusion in the vicinity, is a charming one indeed![4]

'Bourne House' was therefore, the first dwelling to be built in what would one day become Bournemouth. But who built the house? Probably Benjamin Clerke, who was Lord of the Manor of Westover until his death in 1758. And what was the identity of the decoy man? A document compiled by Sir George Tapps in 1790, prior to various sales of land and property made by him to Sir George Rose, refers to a 'Dwelling house & 25 acres of heath and moor land, formerly a Decoy Pond, in Boorn [Bourne] Bottom.' The tenant at that time, who was recorded as having occupied the house since 'Pre-1781', was one Edward Beak.[5] Could Beak, therefore, have been the decoy man?

The Tapps (subsequently Tregonwell) Arms. (Reproduced by permission of Bournemouth Libraries)

There was also an inn nearby – the Tapps Arms – built by Tapps in 1809, and situated just to the east of The Square (on present day Old Christchurch Road). A place of refreshment for those travelling between Iford and Poole, it was also, allegedly, the haunt of smugglers! Elsewhere, at nearby Pokesdown, was Stourfield House, built around 1766 by barrister Edmund Bott, and at Boscombe, Honeycomb Cottage, built by Philip Norris.

Lady Tapps died on 11 July 1813. Tapps himself died on 15 March 1835, when his estate passed to his only son, George William Tapps.

2

Lewis and Henrietta Tregonwell

Lewis Dymoke Grosvenor Tregonwell and his second wife Henrietta, may justly be regarded as the founders of Bournemouth.

The Tregonwells originated from Cornwall, where they were farmers. A notable ancestor was Sir John Tregonwell (*c.* 1498-1565), a lawyer and an ecclesiastical administrator who rose to prominence in the reign of King Henry VIII, and who was largely responsible for steering through Parliament the complicated procedure involved in the dissolution of the King's marriage to Catherine of Aragon. He later drafted legislation concerning the Dissolution of the Monasteries. However, he disapproved of the Church of England's secession from the Church of Rome, and assisted Queen Mary in her attempts to return it to the Roman fold, for which service he received a knighthood.

Lewis, the son of Thomas Tregonwell of Winterborne Anderson, Dorset, was born on 14 February 1758. When he was three years old his father died, leaving him all his property, not only in Anderson but also in Winterborne Kingston and Bloxworth (both in Dorset), and also in Cornwall.

Having attended Oxford University, Tregonwell was appointed High Sheriff of Dorset at the young age of twenty-two. On 11 November 1781 he married Katherine, daughter of wealthy landowner St Barbe Sydenham of The Priory, Broadhembury, Devon, and of Combe House, Brushford, near Dulverton, Somerset, and his wife Ellery (née Williams).

According to Tregonwell's kinsman and contemporary, Dr G.F. Sydenham:

> Some people say Mrs Sydenham advertised her daughter [Katherine, then aged 24 years] … for a fortune of £100,000 a golden bait, and I believe that he [Tregonwell] was the first that did attempt that, she being always under her mother's apron strings and unacquainted with life…[1]

Tregonwell was successful, and in the marriage settlement the couple were granted £500 per annum, together with a house, 'not far off'. The Tregonwells had two (surviving) children: St Barbe (junior, born 6 August 1782) and Helen Ellery (born 12 December 1783). Despite the generosity of Katherine's parents, the couple were not satisfied and made continual demands on them for money – demands that the Sydenhams were unwilling to meet. Finally, in 1787, and presumably out of pique, Tregonwell took his wife and family off to France.

Captain Lewis
Tregonwell by Thomas
Beach. (By kind
permission of Julia
E. Smith)

Having heard that St Barbe Sydenham had made a new will, 'giving all to his wife Mrs Sydenham, excepting £300 for her daughter Katherine', Tregonwell, who had now returned to England, 'formed the following scheme':

They got a chaise and men on horseback with fire-arms to lay hide incog. [incognito] some days. Mr Tregonwell and companion, they went to the The Priory to demand £500 [from the Sydenhams] to pay off some mortgage.

Tregonwell's companion then lured St Barbe Sydenham to his front door, and:

… showing him the chaise in the walk [walkway] … said, 'In that chaise is your daughter and your grandson. Would you not be glad to see them?'

St Barbe acquiesced, and was bundled into the chaise, which quickly drove off. Meanwhile Tregonwell:

… locked the door with Mrs Sydenham in the parlour… Then, having thrown the footman into the pantry, he, went to the stable, took his horse, and went after the chaise.

Her husband having been kidnapped, Mrs Sydenham served Tregonwell with a writ. The case was heard at Exeter Assizes, where Mr Justice Buller asked St Barbe, 'Do you choose to live with Mrs Sydenham or with your son [in-law] and daughter?' He answered the latter. The Justice said, 'Madam, there is no more I can do for you. Mr Sydenham has the right to live with whom he pleases'.

Thereafter, Mrs Sydenham was permitted to continue to live at The Priory with an allowance of £500 per year. As for Tregonwell, 'By this stratagem [he] got £20,000 in cash and about £2,000 a year in fee into his own, or the hands of those whom he chose should have it in trust for him and his children.[2]

With his ill-gotten gains Tregonwell was now able to purchase Cranborne Lodge and Estate at Cranborne in Dorset, where he lived as a country squire with his family and father-in-law, St Barbe.

In 1794, when war with France seemed likely, Tregonwell, with himself as Captain, raised a troop of militia at Cranborne, to serve with the Dorset Volunteer Rangers whose Colonel Commandant was George, Viscount Milton. The Rangers were composed, 'solely of Gentlemen, Yeomen, and respectable Tradesmen', who were, 'Engaged to serve in case of riots and tumults, in any part of the adjoining counties; and in case of invasion, in any part of Great Britain'.

They were to report to their Commanding Officer 'in order to be trained and exercised, not oftener than two days in the week, and not during the time of Harvest or Sheep Shearing'.[3] In the event, war between Britain and France did not commence until May 1803.

Tregonwell was subsequently joined by his son St Barbe, who served as Lieutenant. His brief was to patrol the stretch of coast between Poole and Bourne Chine, and a hinterland stretching as far as Wimborne and Ringwood – a total area of approximately thirty square miles. It should be noted that its easternmost portion, between Alum Chine and Bournemouth, was then part of the county of Hampshire.

Tregonwell's wife Katherine, died in February 1795 aged thirty-eight, and was buried on 21st of that month at Anderson. In November 1799, her father, St Barbe Sydenham, died aged seventy-five, and was buried on 15th of that month at Dulverton, Somerset. As for Tregonwell, he continued in his extravagant lifestyle. Now a Deputy Lieutenant of Dorset, he numbered among his acquaintances the Prince Regent (later King George IV), with whom he spent time hunting, dining, and drinking.

In 1800, Tregonwell was re-married to Henrietta, daughter of another wealthy Dorset landowner, Henry William Portman, Esquire of Orchard Portman and Bryanston, and his wife Ann. In 1802, he retired from the Dorset Volunteer Rangers, the threat of invasion having passed and the Peace Treaty having been signed with France. In that year, the couple had a daughter, Henrietta Lewina.

In 1807, the Tregonwells had a son, Grosvenor Portman, who died in infancy. As a result of this tragedy, Henrietta became deeply depressed. In an attempt to restore his wife's 'former contentment and happy equilibrium', Tregonwell took her every summer for a prolonged visit to Mudeford near Christchurch – a popular spa and centre for sea bathing. On 14 July 1810, the couple took a nostalgic journey westwards from that place, across the heathland to the east of that which he had previously patrolled. When they arrived at a place where a stream called the Bourne reached the sea (which Tregonwell referred to as

The Mansion (subsequently Exeter House), the Tregonwell's seaside retreat.
(Reproduced by permission of Bournemouth Libraries)

'Sandy Mouth'), Henrietta decided that this would be the perfect location for a summer residence. To this end, Tregonwell approached the landowner, Sir George Ivison Tapps, from whom he purchased a parcel of land eight-and-a-half acres in size (and bordering the east side of what is now Exeter Road) for the sum of £179 11s 0d.

The building of the Tregonwell's house at Bourne commenced in March 1811. On 26 September of that year, Henrietta gave birth to another son, John. On 24 April 1812, the house (originally known as 'The Mansion'), which was a three-storey gabled structure with superb views of the sea, was ready for occupation. That day, Henrietta noted in her diary, 'Went to Bourne. Slept there for the first time'. From now on, the family divided its time between Bourne and Anderson.

The Tregonwell Estate plan of around 1835, the key to which has been lost, depicts a property standing on its own and situated immediately to the west of The Mansion. It is also depicted on a painting, executed by Julia E. Smith (namesake of the current owner of Edmonsham House) shortly after the arrival of the Tregonwells in the area. Furthermore, subsequent plans reveal that this property was called 'The Priory' – which was the name of St Barbe Sydenham's former abode in Devonshire. Surely this was not a coincidence?

To the north of The Mansion, Tregonwell built a four-roomed thatched cottage for his butler, Thomas Symes – which was known as Symes's Cottage. He subsequently purchased further portions of land from Tapps, and also the Tapps Arms, which in 1832 was rebuilt and renamed the Tregonwell Arms. Tregonwell's final purchase, made in 1822, was of land to the north-west of The Mansion. Here, he built Prospect (later Terrace) Mount, a cottage for his gardener.

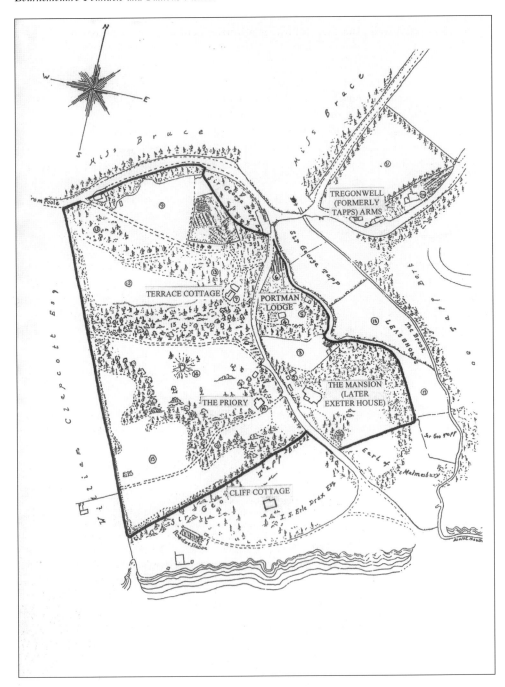

The Tregonwell Estate, Bourne (possibly by Thomas Bennett, the estate surveyor), *c.* 1835.

In 1820, Tregonwell placed the following advertisement in a local newspaper:

A MARINE RESIDENCE LOOKING TO THE SEA

TO BE LET (furnished)

A modern, detached, convenient HOUSE at Bourne Mouth, midway between Poole and Christchurch, consisting of three parlours, 16ft and 17ft. each, nearly square, fronting the sea, six or seven bedrooms, kitchen, scullery, housekeeper's room, servants' hall, larder, etc. Also a coach-house, stable for two horses, a garden full cropped, a well of good water, and a bathing machine. The situation is particularly airy and healthy, in the centre of a fine open bay between Christchurch Head and Branksea [Brownsea] Castle [at the mouth of Poole Harbour]; there is an easy approach to a very beautiful beach of several miles extent. The house stands on a green near the high road and a small Inn, where carriers stop daily on their way to the two nearest market towns. A butcher and baker will bring provisions. Cows are kept on the spot... [5]

Who could possibly resist such a property? Certainly not the Marchioness of Exeter, who promptly took out a lease on The Mansion. It was from her that its subsequent name, Exeter House, derived. Since their former abode was now permanently let, the Tregonwells enlarged Terrace Mount (which became Terrace Cottage), and made this their family home instead.

Terrace Cottage, *c.* 1865.
(Fraser Donachie)

Great friends of the Tregonwells were the Drax Grosvenors of Charborough, Dorset, who, by 1815, were in possession of Cliff Cottage, a seaside retreat situated on the west side of the lower part of Exeter Road, on land which they owned between the Tregonwell Estate and the sea.

Nineteenth-century English diarist and social observer Harriet Arbuthnot, in her journal, gives a graphic account of a visit she made to the area on 11 August 1824:

> I rode one day to a place called Bournemouth which are a collection of hills lately planted by a gentleman of the name of Tregunwell, who has built four or five beautiful cottages which he lets to persons who go for sea bathing. I was so charmed with the beauty of the situation that Mr. A. [her husband] and I have half agreed to take one next summer for the sake of a little bathing.[6]

Harriet may be forgiven for misspelling Tregonwell's name, for this was the way in which it was originally pronounced! Thousands were eventually to follow in Tregonwell's and his wife Harriet's wake.

Tregonwell died on 18 January 1832 aged seventy-three years, and was buried at Anderson. He was succeeded by his elder son St Barbe, who inherited Anderson Manor. Meanwhile, younger brother John, inherited Cranborne Lodge.

On 26 February 1846, Henrietta had her late husband's remains (and also the remains of their infant son, Grosvenor), transferred from Anderson to a specially erected vault in the churchyard of St Peter's Church, Bournemouth. She now made Symes's Cottage her home and renamed it Portman Lodge, Portman being her maiden name.

On 15 April 1846, Henrietta herself died, aged seventy-nine, and was interred in the family vault, which is aptly inscribed with the following words:

> Bournemouth, which Mr Tregonwell was the first to bring into notice as a Watering place by erecting a mansion for his own occupation, having been his favourite retreat for many years before his death.

His wife Henrietta, however, as already mentioned, must share the credit with him, for being the co-founder of modern-day Bournemouth, and they may be justly accredited not only with founding Bournemouth, but also with creating the first holiday accommodation in the area. However, it was not for holidaymakers that Bournemouth was first primarily intended, as will soon be seen.

Bourne House (or the Decoy House), the first residential property in Bournemouth, was shown still to be in existence on John Cary's map of Hampshire, dated 1825.

In 1837, George Fox had purchased the Tregonwell Arms from Lewis Tregonwell's widow, Henrietta. In 1839, the inn was appointed Receiving Office for letters posted to Bournemouth; with Fox serving both as inn proprietor and as Bournemouth's first postmaster. In 1840, a daily post was established between Bournemouth and Poole.

The Tregonwell Estate Account Book 1846-84, which was kept meticulously by Lewis and Henrietta's son John, of Cranborne Lodge, shows life continuing very much as before, with income being derived from the renting out of land and property. For example, rents accrued from Portman Cottage (Lodge); Terrace Cottage (part of which was evidently let), farm, paddock, meadow, and garden allotment; the cottage at The Priory's stables;

Portman Lodge, *c.* 1875. (Fraser Donachie)

Bournemouth, shortly after the arrival of the Tregonwells, depicting 'The Mansion' (left) and
'The Priory' (right). (Mrs Julia E. Smith)

Baverstock Cottage (not identified), together with a farm and yet more cottages which the Tregonwells owned at Moordown. On 24 June 1851, John Tregonwell received £1 10s, 'of C. Sweatland for 1,000 furze faggots'.

Further entries show that visitors to Bourne were not only able to rent the Tregonwell cottages, but also to avail themselves of meals and hospitality:

> 1 July 1846. Recd [Received] of Capt. Popham for breakfast at Terrace Cottage 3s.1d.
>
> 23 March 1847. Recd of Mr Monroe for breakfast at Exeter House 8s.4d.

Exeter House may, therefore, be described as Bournemouth's first boarding house. Outgoings included the following:

> 6 June 1846. For sweeping all the chimneys at the Mansion £1.6s.0d. [In the same month, payments were made for] Beer for men while mowing and hay making★ [Tregonwell's spelling - together with] gravel, thatch, and corn.
>
> 18 July 1846. Pew rents at the church £5.0.0.
>
> 1 August 1846. For hire of horse to Salisbury 12s.
>
> 1 September 1846. Char woman★ 7 days at Exeter House 6s.
>
> 5 September 1846. For repairing thatch at Portman Cottage 5s.
>
> October 1847. Giles Sweetapple, mole catcher, one year £1.
>
> August 1848. Paid 2s for cow at Parkstone Pound.
>
> 27 June 1847. Postage Stamps 6s.
>
> 6 August 1849. Repairing clocks 12/6.
>
> 10 September 1849. Cleaning windows (Butler) 1/6.
>
> 27 April 1851. Shaking carpet at Portman Lodge 2s.

There were further outgoings in respect of the wider community:

> 3 June 1849. Easter offerings to clergymen 10s.
>
> 12 December 1846. Pd [Paid] policeman 2s.
>
> September 1849. Subscription to school £1 [and] subscription to choir 10s.
>
> 2 July 1847. Poor rate to Holdenhurst Parish £7.16s 5d. [The Poor Rate being a tax levied on property, the proceeds being used to provide relief for the poor of the parish.]

In 1846, John Tregonwell was appointed one of Bournemouth's thirteen Commissioners (q.v.).

From about 1858, the Reverend J.H. Wanklyn occupied Exeter House – where he ran a private preparatory school for boys.[7] In 1867, Tregonwell became a trustee of Bournemouth's proposed new Church of Holy Trinity. He died in 1885.

When Portman Lodge was demolished in 1930, suspicions were raised that Lewis Tregonwell had been involved with smuggling. This was because a secret chamber was found beneath the house, with access by way of a trap door.

Tregonwell's former estate is today at the heart of modern-day Bournemouth, and his former house, The Mansion, now forms the central part of the Royal Exeter Hotel in Exeter Road.

3

Sir George William Tapps Gervis (2nd Baronet)

George William Tapps, born on 24 March 1795, was the only son of Sir George Ivison Tapps of Hinton Admiral. On 26 September 1825 he married Clara Meyrick Fuller, eldest daughter of Augustus Eliott Fuller MP of Rosehill Park, Sussex, and his wife, Clara (née Meyrick). In 1835, Tapps assumed the additional names and arms of Gervis, thus becoming Sir George William Tapps Gervis.

It was the ambition of Gervis, MP for New Romney in Kent and subsequently, from 1832-37, for Christchurch in Dorset, to create at Bourne Mouth (the name Bournemouth dates from 1840) a marine village which would rival Weymouth in Dorset, or Brighton in Sussex. In the words of J. Sydenham, author of *The Visitor's Guide to Bournemouth and its Neighbourhood*, Gervis:

> being the principal landowner in the neighbourhood… became satisfied that Bournemouth was endowed by nature with especial features and circumstances which eminently fitted it to become an approved resort of those, who, at the termination of the London season, seek on the coast that invigorating repose, and that commixture of fashion and retirement, which afford the best protection against ennui, and are most conducive to the restoration of that freshness and activity, both in the physical and mental functions which the constant excitement of town life have as great a tendency to undermine.

To this end, Gervis commissioned Benjamin Ferrey (q.v.), a young architect from nearby Christchurch, to plan and oversee the development of his Westover Estate. It is the view of Sir George Gervis (7th Baronet), that just as the Tregonwells may be regarded as the founders of Bournemouth, so Sir George W.T. Gervis may be regarded as its father.

Continuing the family tradition of promoting Christianity in the area, Gervis bore the entire cost of creating Bournemouth's St Peter's Church, the foundation stone of which was laid on 28 September 1841. Prior to this, services had been held in temporary premises in The Square, in a pair of semi-detached cottages which had been made into one and substantially modified. With the opening of St Peter's, these premises were retained as a schoolroom for the National Day School, and also as a Sunday school. Gervis also donated the land upon which the Reverend Morden Bennett, Vicar of St Peter's Church, Bournemouth, erected a chapel/school at Moordown, designed by the young ecclesiastical architect George Edmund Street – who achieved fame by designing London's prestigious Law Courts.

St Peter's Church (designed
by John Tulloch), April 1855.
(Fraser Donachie)

Early Bournemouth by Julia E. Smith. (Mrs Julia E. Smith)

Gervis, however, did not live to see St Peter's Church completed, for he died on 26 August 1842 at the age of forty-seven, his wife having died a decade earlier on 27 December 1831.

The untimely death of Gervis brought the work of building St Peter's Church to a halt – no formal contract having been entered into. As Gervis's son was a mere infant, it was left to the Gervis trustees to resolve the matter, which they did in the Court of Chancery, whose favourable decision enabled them to complete and endow the property. The church, designed by architect John Tulloch of Poole and Wimborne, was finally licensed for services and opened in the summer of 1844. Some have described the building as ugly, but a depiction of it in *The Visitor's Guide to Bournemouth* does not bear this out.

4

Benjamin Ferrey

Benjamin Ferrey was a young and talented local architect whose plans for Bournemouth were both ambitious and imaginative. The question was, would these plans come to fruition? The Ferreys were of French Huguenot (Calvinist Protestant) descent, who probably emigrated to England following a series of religious wars which took place in France in the second half of the sixteenth century.

Ferrey was born on 1 April 1810 at Christchurch, where his father, Benjamin senior of Castle Street, was Master of the Leper Hospital of St Mary Magdalen (and who, in 1840, became Mayor of the town). Having been educated at Wimborne Grammar School, Ferrey was articled to architect Augustus Pugin, father of the more famous architect Augustus Welby Northmore Pugin, and subsequently in 1834 set up on his own account in Great Russell Street, London. In the same year, with co-author Edward Wedlake Brayley, he published his *Antiquities of the Priory Church of Christchurch, Hampshire*. He also carried out restoration work on the medieval priory. In 1836, he married Ann, daughter of Mr Lucas of Stapleton Hall, Hornsey, Middlesex. The couple had three children, Alicia, Benjamin Edward and Annie.

Having been commissioned in 1836 by Sir George Gervis, Ferrey now set about designing 'the marine resort of Bournemouth'. This was his first commission and he threw himself into it with gusto. His ambitious and grandiose schemes included the construction of rows of detached villas which would snake, in a serpentine fashion, along the slopes overlooking the Bourne Chine and along the East Cliff. There would also be a new pier and a roundabout at the top of Bath Hill, complete with obelisk!

Dr Augustus B. Granville MD, FRS, asked in his book, entitled *The Spas of England*, whether it was necessary or desirable:

> … to try to cover in concentric circles the whole face of the hill…with lines of lodging and
> other dwelling houses, and crowning the whole with a Gothic church, placed in the centre of
> the summit, like a diadem…

This was clearly intended as a criticism of Ferrey, one of whose lithographs (executed by George Barnard) depicted exactly such a proposal. Continued Granville:

> … it will not do for invalids with delicate chests and damaged lungs to climb up to the
> Capitol, either [in order] to return home after a walk on the sea-shore, or to attend at church
> on a Sunday, to be blown away in endeavouring to reach the House of God…[1]

Benjamin Ferrey. (Courtesy of RIBA Library
Photograph Collection)

Despite such strictures, however, Ferrey made his mark, even though many of his
plans failed to come to fruition, and others were scaled down. The outcome was that,
between 1837 and 1841, Westover Villas, comprising sixteen properties built to his
design and each standing in its own grounds, appeared in what would later become
Westover Road.

He also designed the Bath Hotel and the Belle Vue Boarding House. Adjoining the
latter were, 'the commodious and spacious reading-rooms and library, well supplied with
the London and provincial newspapers and periodicals; the library consists of several
hundreds of standard and useful works'.[2] Both the Bath Hotel and the Belle View
Boarding House, which were designed for those visitors, 'who preferred and required a
quieter mode of life',[3] were opened by Gervis on Queen Victoria's Coronation Day – 28
June 1838. In about 1850, the Belle Vue Boarding House became the Belle Vue and Pier
Hotel. A number of villas, also designed by Ferrey, were erected on the East Cliff. However,
his design for a church was rejected.

In *The Visitor's Guide to Bournemouth and its Neighbourhood*, first published in 1840, the
following eulogy appeared in praise of Ferrey's creations:

Thus on spots where, before, the foot of man rarely pressed, but the lowly heath flower
blossomed and faded in unnoticed solitude, where no sound was heard but the rustling of
the rank grass and the wild shrub, as they waved in the light sea-breeze, - there a number of
detached villas, each marked by distinct and peculiar architectural features, have sprung into
existence, affording accommodation of varying extent, so as to be suited to the convenience
of either large or small families... To all these are attached ample gardens, whilst in the front
are shrubberies [and] tastefully laid out walks arranged with due regard for convenience and
effect. At one end of this range stands a spacious and commodious hotel (The Bath Hotel),
erected for the accommodation of more temporary visitants, and fitted up in the most

St Peter's Church, Westover Villas and the Bath Hotel. (From an engraving by H. Burn, reproduced by permission of Bournemouth Libraries)

Nos 1 and 2, Western (Westover) Villas. (Fraser Donachie)

The Bath Hotel,
c. 1845. (Reproduced
by permission of
Bournemouth
Libraries)

The West Cliff, *c.* 1845. (Reproduced by permission of Bournemouth Libraries)

Bournemouth from the water, *c.* 1850. (Engraving by Phillip Brannon)

complete style. All these edifices command views of the ocean, of the distant coast, and of the vale lying immediately beneath, whilst the site is, at the same time, as judiciously chosen, that they are effectively sheltered from the biting [wind] of the north and east.

In 1841, Ferrey was appointed Honorary Architect to the Diocese of Bath and Wells, a position which he held until his death. During his later years he continued with his creative activities: designing churches, a grammar school, and a college, and laying out parks at various locations in England.

In 1861, Ferrey published his *Recollections of A.N. Welby Pugin and his father Augustus Pugin* (whose pupil he had once been). One of the earliest members of the Royal Institute of British Architects (founded in 1834 and which received its Royal Charter in 1837), he served twice as its Vice President, and in 1870 was awarded that organization's Royal Gold Medal. He died on 22 August 1880 at his London home.

Sir George Eliott Meyrick Tapps Gervis Meyrick (3rd Baronet)

Sir George Gervis's son, Sir George Eliott Meyrick Tapps Gervis, was born on 1 September 1827. He shared his father's (Sir George W.T. Gervis) aspirations for Bournemouth, and in 1845, had the brilliant notion of appointing Decimus Burton to succeed Benjamin Ferrey as architect to the Gervis Estate. As previously mentioned, Burton was already known to the family, having previously advised the 1st Baronet on the layout of his London estate.

Burton was duly engaged, and in 1845, in a report addressed to the estate solicitor G.A. Crawley, he outlined his vision for the town. Said he:

> The wooded valley through which the Bourne rivulet flows to the sea is and must always constitute the principal object in the landscape, and therefore any work undertaken there should be most jealously watched, and every endeavour made to preserve the natural beauty of the valley.

It was Bournemouth's rusticity, he said, which would attract, 'a class of visitors…who cannot find the same elsewhere'.[1] Burton now proceeded to make his mark on Bournemouth, as will shortly be seen.

On 4 December 1849, Gervis married Fanny, daughter of Christopher Harland of Ashbourne, Derbyshire. Bournemouth's first Town Hall was erected on the site of what later became the Criterion Arcade (situated to the east of The Square), by the Bournemouth Town Hall Company. It was opened by Gervis and his wife on 6 January 1875. Following family tradition, Gervis provided land for the chapel/school to be built at Moordown, and for the Anglican Church of St James the Greater to be built at Pokesdown. In 1876, he assumed the additional name and arms of Meyrick, thus becoming Sir George Eliott Meyrick Tapps Gervis Meyrick. In the 1890s, 'Sir George Meyrick, Bart' is listed as being one of the Vice Presidents of Bournemouth's National Sanatorium (q.v.). He died on 7 April 1896.

Sir George Eliott Meyrick Tapps Gervis Meyrick. (Sir George Meyrick)

Decimus Burton

Son of James Burton of London, architect and builder, Decimus Burton was born on 30 September 1800. He came to Bournemouth in August 1845, where his role as architect to the Gervis Estate was one of advisor, planner, and overseer, rather than that of designer of buildings. However, from correspondence with the trustees, it is clear that certain stipulations were made with regard to the quality and positioning of the buildings that were to be erected on the Gervis Estate.

Burton first trained in the practice of his father, and subsequently under notable architect John Nash, who was responsible for the layout of much of Regency London. Burton became known not only as an architect of such buildings as churches, hospitals, and gentlemen's clubs, but also as a creator of parks and gardens, and of complete seaside towns! In particular, with iron-founder Richard Turner, he designed the glass and iron Palm House at Kew, which in the late 1840s, was the largest of its kind in the world. He also designed buildings at London Zoo, including the Llama House and the Giraffe House, and was responsible for planning the layout of Hyde Park, including the Wellington Arch at Hyde Park Corner (built to commemorate the Duke of Wellington's victories in the Napoleonic Wars).

In a letter written to the Trustees of the Gervis Estate from his London home, 6 Spring Garden, on 26 September 1845, Burton presented his thoughts as to what the future of Bournemouth might be:

Dear Sir,

As desired by you I proceeded to Bournemouth on the 7th August last, and again on the 16th instant, for the purpose of surveying the portions of the Gervis estate lying near that watering place, and of making a general report upon the subject with reference to letting these lands for building.

I shall make no comments upon the attractions that Bournemouth possesses in scenery, climate, bathing sands, &c; because, I believe these are universally acknowledged and appreciated by all that have visited the spot – I reported to this effect in the year 1840 when I visited the place at the instance of Mr Gordon [William Gordon, owner of land in the vicinity of Richmond Hill]. Building only to a small extent has been carried on since that period. A few small houses have been erected on the Poole Road. Nearly all the lodgings and the two hotels [the Exeter and the Bath] are at this time full and I am assured that there is a demand for more accommodation, and that houses of a large scale are particularly enquired for, from it which may be agreed that the place is in good repute with the higher classes.

Decimus Burton, lithograph after a drawing by Eden Upton Ellis, 1832. (Hastings Museum & Art Gallery)

The site for each house should be designated and adhered to, reference in the selection being had to the preservation to each to the views of the sea or Landscape. There should be covenants in the leases to prevent obstruction of these views by additional buildings or growth of trees.

Caution should be used in thinning the present Plantations, to preserve all the best grown trees, with reference rather to their beauty of form, than to their value in the market.

New roads were to be 'formed' [i.e. created] complete with the provision of fencing, gates, and drainage, and properties were to be screened from each other by foliage. This included Upper Road, Middle Road, Lower Road and the north-west end of Westover Road. Burton also proposed that on the cliff top, walks, drives, and a wide, gravelled path be constructed. Said he:

After the roads shall have been formed at the cost of the trustees [of the Gervis estate] I think that £10 per acre, per annum, may at the present time be set down as a fair average rent for the land on the Cliff and for that in the immediate vicinity of the place… [1]

The lower end of the Bourne Valley was to be laid out as an ornamental pleasure ground, which would extend from the seafront to the bridge on the Poole Road, in what is now The Square. This project finally came to fruition in 1873, at about which time the meadows above the bridge were converted, by permission of George Durrant, owner of the Branksome Estate, into the Upper Pleasure Gardens. In total, the Pleasure Gardens comprised about twenty-nine acres.

As for what Dr Augustus B. Granville referred to as, 'the present insignificant wooden bridge', Burton, in 1848, advocated, 'the erection of a carriage bridge over the Bourne Stream, and the formation of the road through Mr. Tregonwell's property to the Poole Road'. The work was completed in the following year, the bridge having been constructed in brick by David Tuck, building contractor to the Gervis Estate.

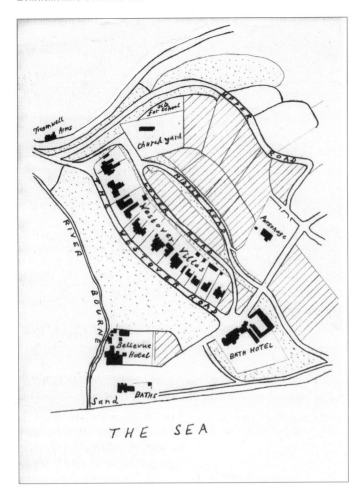

Bournemouth (after plan referred to in Mr Decimus Burton's report dated 21 August 1847). The roads which were 'proposed to be formed' included Upper Road, Middle Road, Lower Road and the north-west end of Westover Road. The dotted ground is 'proposed to be planted and laid out as public promenades.' The hatched ground is 'to be let for building.'

In 1847, Burton met a deputation of prominent local residents, to hear proposals for the erection of a pier or jetty. The outcome was that in July 1855, the first piles for the new jetty were driven in by contractor, Samuel Ingram. Complete with a retractable platform, the jetty served its purpose from 1856 to 1861, when Bournemouth's new (wooden) pier was opened, in the presence of Sir George and Lady Gervis.

In 1858, following negotiations with the Gervis Estate, a walkway was created through Westover Gardens – a pine wood situated between Westover Road and the Bourne. Originally known as 'Invalid's Walk', this was subsequently renamed 'Pine Walk'. Just over a decade later, in July 1869, Sir George E.M.T. Gervis consented to footpaths being made on either side of the Bourne.

As for Burton, he became a Fellow of the Royal Society and was one of the earliest members of the Royal Institute of British Architects. He never married. He died on 14 December 1881 and is buried alongside his father in the churchyard of West Hill Road, St Leonards, East Sussex, a town designed almost entirely by his father, where he had spent his last few years.

Dr Augustus Bozzi Granville

Italian surgeon, physician, and writer Dr Augustus Granville, of 5 Cornwall Terrace, Warwick Square, London, first visited Bournemouth in February 1841, when he found lodgings at one of the newly erected villas in Westover Road. He was there, in his words, to fulfil a 'medical engagement' in the neighbourhood, and at the same time, to accept an invitation from, 'several gentlemen connected with that almost unknown sea-watering-place, to visit and give my professional opinion respecting it'.[1]

Granville, born Augustus Bozzi in Milan on 7 October 1783, was the third son of Carlo Bozzi, Postmaster General of the Lombardo-Austrian Provinces. Having graduated as Doctor of Medicine from Padua in 1802, he fled Italy, which was currently occupied by the forces of Napoleon Bonaparte. In a life of adventure, he served with the Turkish fleet as second physician, practised medicine in Spain (prior to which he took a qualifying examination in Latin) and became an honorary member of the Royal Academy of Medicine in Madrid. Bozzi arrived in the Portuguese capital of Lisbon on Christmas Day 1806, where he discovered a British naval squadron in port. He was duly appointed Assistant Surgeon (and later Surgeon) to the Royal Navy sloop of war, HMS *Raven*. In 1809 he married a Miss Kerr, daughter of Joseph Kerr of Blackheath, Surrey.

Bozzi retired from the Royal Navy in 1813 and settled in London. He mastered the English language and assisted the Foreign Office in interpreting and translating. He became a lecturer in chemistry at St George's Hospital Medical School, and studied at Westminster Hospital. In that year he was admitted to membership of The Royal College of Surgeons. In 1814, when he assumed the name 'Granville' – after his maternal grandmother Rosa Granville, who was English, he relocated temporarily to Paris to study midwifery.

In 1817, Granville, as he now was, became Licentiate of the Royal College of Physicians, and set up in practice in London at 8 Savile Row. He became editor of the *Medical Intelligencer*, and then of the *London Medical and Physical Journal*. In 1819 he published his *Report on the Practice of Midwifery*, and in 1820, learned papers on the stethoscope (invented by French physician René Laënnec in 1816) and on *The Internal Use of Hydrocyanic Acid in Pulmonary Consumption*. Here, it should be mentioned that 'consumption' was the former name for tuberculosis. The name was appropriate, since the disease seemed to consume the sufferer from within, causing a relentless wasting of the body. The disease was recognized by the ancient Greeks who called it phthisis. In England in 1815, one death in four was due to consumption.

Granville was an advocate of the benefits of spas and sea bathing in the promotion of health, and in 1837, published *The Spas of Germany* in two volumes. He would go on to publish

Dr Augustus Bozzi Granville. (Copyright: Royal College of Physicians of London)

The Mineral Springs of Vichy, in 1859. By now, word of his interest and influence in this field had spread to Bournemouth, and to mark the occasion of his visit to the town in 1841, a public dinner was given in his honour at the Bath Hotel, 'in a style of excellence seldom surpassed even in the metropolis'. Dr Granville, for his part, responded by making the following speech:

> I have examined Bourne in all its parts, under sunshine as well as during the prevalence of wet and high wind. I have seen what has been done, and have heard of what is intended to do, in order to profit of the many advantages which the situation of Bourne offers as a watering-place; and I have no hesitation in stating… that no situation that I have had occasion to examine along the whole of the southern coast, possesses so many capabilities of being made the very first invalid sea-watering place in England; and not only a watering place, but what is still more important, a winter residence for the most delicate constitutions requiring a warm and sheltered locality at this season of the year.
>
> In fact, gentlemen, you have a spot here which you may convert into a perfect blessing to those among the wealthy who are sorely afflicted with disease, and who do not like to tear themselves from home to go in search of foreign and salubrious climates.[2]

The 'several gentlemen' who had invited Granville to Bournemouth were gratified by his visit. They were even more gratified when he devoted no less than twenty-one pages to the town in his volume, *The Spas of England and Principal Sea-Bathing Places: Southern Spas*, which was published later in that year, 1841 (as the second of three volumes). In it, he set out his thoughts in greater detail:

I look upon Bournemouth, and its yet unformed colony [i.e. settlement], as a perfect discovery among the sea-nooks one longs to have for a real invalid, and as the realization of a desideratum we vainly thought to have found ourselves on the south coast of England.[3]

As an authority on tuberculosis, Granville's remarks carried considerable weight. Furthermore, this was a disease which led to many of those who suffered from it becoming 'invalids' – an appellation which was in common use at the time.

He then explained, in detail, how his view of Bournemouth had been arrived at. Firstly, he paid tribute to the late Lewis Tregonwell, who had planted, 'all the sandhills to the westward of the Bourne, or brook, with trees of the Pine tribe [variety], whereby the district has been converted, in the course of time, into a sort of tiny Black Forest [in Germany]'. Secondly, he had discovered, 'three or four retired glens' [presumably a reference to the chines], where the temperature, during cold conditions was, 'from eight to ten degrees higher than on the table-land', and he had personally taken measurements with his thermometer to confirm that this was the case. The patient would then, after, 'issuing from his glen', be able to inhale the, 'invigorating breeze', before returning to his retreat, 'there to enjoy immunity from severe or brisk atmosphere…'. Finally, he requested that Dr Aitken, 'the scientific and pains-taking physician of Poole', should examine the chemical composition of the water in the brook [Bourne] – which the latter did, and confirmed that it was pure and uncontaminated.[4]

Having ascertained the facts, Granville was now in a position to make his recommendations. Many more houses must be built in order to create 'a regular community of village', to which those with 'all the necessary arts and trades' would be encouraged to come.[5] Both the East and West Cliffs were sites where summer residences 'might advantageously be erected', whether singly or as a parade. In addition, he advocated the building of a church.

Granville also had ideas for the Bourne, observing that:

The little brook itself, perfectly wild, shallow and tortuous, and with no great width, meanders down the middle [of the valley]; but a little judicious management, by swelling out the banks in parts, contracting them in others, and deepening the bed here, or raising it there, so as to create a rustling fall or cascade, would readily convert an insignificant streamlet into a pleasing ornamental water feature in the landscape. The garden, with suitable gravel walks, would afford to the weakest and most delicate among the real invalids at Bournemouth the means of taking exercise on foot whenever any other wind but the north prevails…[6]

He concluded his address by telling the assembled gentlemen of Bournemouth, 'I have pointed out to you… all that is requisite to be done, to make the place perfect, and it will be your own fault if Bourne is not soon an object of general admiration and attraction'.

Having had so fulsome an endorsement – both in his speech and in his book – from such an eminent, authoritative, and renowned person as Dr Granville, all that remained was for the gentlemen of Bournemouth to put his ideas into effect!

When Granville's wife died in 1861, he gave up his London practice. In 1871, he moved to Dover, where he himself died on 3 March 1872.

The Reverend Alexander Morden Bennett

In the summer of 1845, thirty-six-year-old Reverend Alexander Morden Bennett, assistant priest at Portman Chapel, Baker Street, London, arrived in Bournemouth to be inducted as the town's first Vicar. Six decades later, his son, the Reverend Alexander Sykes Bennett, would recall the occasion – his recollections being reported in the *Bournemouth Graphic*. When the Reverend A.S. Bennett first came to Bournemouth with his father in 1845:

> … there were but 300 people in the 'village' [and] there were no public elementary schools at all. In fact the only school… was a Sunday school, and that was held in a building in what was now called The Square… a building that for some time had been used for divine worship on Sundays. Nor were the scholars very numerous. Indeed, on the first Sunday on which his father [the Reverend A.M. Bennett] drove over from Mudeford [near Christchurch] to enter the duty, so few in number were they that as he walked from the Belle Vue Hotel, where he put up his horse, to the school to open it, he overtook the teacher with the key in one hand and holding the solitary scholar by the other. It was true that there was a church, but it was a very different sort of church from that which now stood on the very same site in the very centre of the town… [i.e. St Peter's.]

The Reverend A.S. Bennett was, however, somewhat scathing about Bournemouth's (first) Church of St Peter, perhaps unjustifiably so, as has already been mentioned:

> Well did he [Alexander] remember that little old church [St Peter's, designed by John Tulloch] with four castellated excrescences, one at each corner of the roof, and the tiny spire. And then inside the western gallery there was the village orchestra sackbut [early form of trombone], psaltery [medieval instrument, like a dulcimer, but played by plucking the strings], and all kinds of music.

And when, on 7 August 1845, Charles Richard Sumner, Bishop of Winchester, came to consecrate the church and the collection plate was handed round, he, Alexander, put into it, 'a bright half sovereign which his grandfather had given him for the purpose'.[1]

Alexander Morden Bennett was born at Morden College, Blackheath, Kent (founded by philanthropist Sir John Morden – to whom he was related by marriage – in 1695 as a home for forty-four merchants who had found themselves in, 'reduced circumstances'). Here, his father and namesake Alexander, was college treasurer.

Bennett's first wife was Maria Sarah, daughter of London parson the Reverend Josiah Pike, by whom he had a son Alexander Sykes Bennett (mentioned above), and a daughter, Elizabeth Ann. However, Maria had died whilst Bennett was serving at Shepton Mallet, Somerset, as temporary priest-in-charge.

Bennett's new position in Bournemouth had several disadvantages. The endowment was a mere £50, and the income from pew rents (whereby pews were rented out to parishioners) was less than £200. Also, there being no parsonage, the new incumbent was expected to build one at his own expense! Bennett's decision to move to Bournemouth, however, may have been influenced by the fact that his second wife's family home was at Christchurch. She was Marianne Elizabeth, daughter of Captain Henry Hopkins, whom he had married in early 1845.

The Reverend Alexander Morden Bennett. (Reproduced by permission of Bournemouth Libraries)

The parsonage, designed by architect Edmund Pearce of Canford Magna and situated on high ground above the church with commanding views over the sea, was not completed until the following year. Meanwhile, Bennett lived temporarily at Mudeford, from where he was obliged to commute across the heathland to Bournemouth.

One of Bennett's first concerns was to raise funds to provide Bournemouth with a school. This he did successfully, and on 30 June 1850, the foundation stone of St Peter's School (which adjoined the church of the same name) was laid by Lady Louisa, wife of the Honourable Walter Ponsonby, Vicar of Canford Magna.

In 1851, Edmund Pearce was commissioned to add an aisle onto the south side of Tulloch's original St Peter's Church, with a vestry at the east end. Its foundation stone was laid by Lady Gervis on 21 May. In the same year, the Bennetts had a son, Henry Morden Bennett.

In the winter of 1851–52, Bennett was struck by a double tragedy. His wife Marianne died on 7 December 1851 aged thirty-seven; and Elizabeth Ann, his daughter by his first wife Maria, died the following month at the age of nine, after a week-long febrile illness. Bennett's congregation responded by presenting to the church two memorial windows, 'as a testimonial of esteem and token of sympathy towards their pastor in a season of severe affliction'. Marianne was buried in the churchyard of St Peter's. Elizabeth Ann's place of burial is not known.

During his thirty-four year incumbency at St Peter's, Bennett established no less than eight outposts of the church in Bournemouth's outlying districts: namely, the Churches of St John, Moordown; St James, Pokesdown; St Barnabas, East Parley; St Michael, Bournemouth; St Clement, Boscombe; St Swithin, Bournemouth; St Aldhelm, Branksome, and St Ambrose, Westbourne. Church schools were also provided. In fact, the following statement, which Bennett subsequently made, reveals that he regarded his role as being akin to that of a missionary:

We have seen in this parish what may be done among a neglected and uncared for population by sending for the ministers to carry to the houses of our poor the glad tidings of the gospel, and the comforts of our Holy Religion as well as to minister the word and sacraments on a Sunday. Beginning often without a building even wherein to hold a service on the Lord's Day, we have seen congregations gathered together on the village green; then a school established, and lastly a school [come] chapel… in which all, from the least to the greatest, may worship God in the beauty of holiness, and after the manner of their forefathers.

There was also a lighter side to life, as this description of what followed a harvest festival thanksgiving service at East Parley indicates:

A brass band, hired from Kinson for the occasion, marched in front of the company assembling in the fields, and then it took up its place in a waggon. A part of the field had been separated off by hurdles so as to form a banqueting hall, where the tables were arranged, and covered with the whitest of cloths, which contrasted well with the bright green carpeting of grass. The tables were shaded from the sun by the trees, which was a most agreeable arrangement. When all had taken their seats, silence was obtained, and the Rev. A.M. Bennett [had] said the grace, and then every one in earnest regaled themselves with tea, cake, and bread and butter, which was most abundantly supplied, and the best of its kind. During the repast, the band played some gay lively tunes – suggestive of dancing – and gradually the tea tables were deserted for that part of the field where the games and amusements were prepared. All the clergy present mixed with and promoted the merry-making.[2]

Bennett described St Peter's Church as, 'a very poor structure', and he was determined to rectify what he considered to be a serious blot on the landscape. Also, he foresaw that the population of Bournemouth was likely to rise rapidly (which it did, there being, according to the census, 695 persons resident there in 1851, and 1,707 a decade later in 1861). He therefore, in 1855, commissioned G.E. Street, Honorary Architect to the Diocese of Oxford – who would become a leading ecclesiastical architect of the day – to convert the building into a 'commodious and beautiful church'.[3]

This was the first time that Street had been commissioned to create (or in this case, adapt) a town church, and he was fortunate in that the benefactors of the project were opulent enough to bear the costs, which were substantial. Nonetheless, the expense of employing some of the finest artists and craftsmen in the land, William Morris and Sir Edward Burne-Jones, for example, was so great that it was found necessary to perform the work in stages. It was completed as follows: in 1856, the north aisle; in 1859, the nave, clerestory, and south porch. The roof of Tulloch's original church was pulled down when the clerestory was built above it. Finally, on Christmas Day 1859, the church was reopened.

Bennett also found time to be involved in the founding of Bournemouth's Volunteer Rifle Corps in 1860, and was chaplain to the volunteer riflemen. In 1863, by which time he had been joined by two assistants – the Reverend S.R. Waddelow and the Reverend James H. Wanklyn – he was also joined by his son, the Reverend A.S. Bennett (who prior to this had been Curate of Wilton, Wiltshire).

In 1864, the chancel and transepts were added, and on 20 December, St Peter's was consecrated by Bishop Sumner. By 1870, the tower had been added, and at Whitsuntide

Above and right:
St Peter's Church,
c. 1865, and *c.* 1870.
(Fraser Donachie)

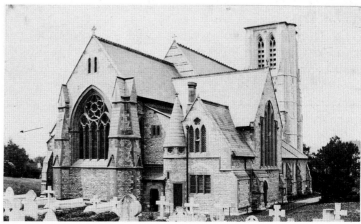

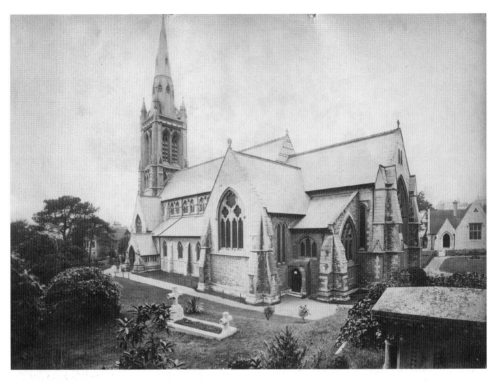

St Peter's – the completed church. (Reproduced by permission of Bournemouth Libraries)

1871, its eight bells, made by Taylors of Loughborough and donated by the inhabitants of Bournemouth, were hung therein, 'To the Glory of God and as a mark of esteem and respect for the Reverend Alexander Morden Bennett MA'. In 1874, work was commenced on the western transepts. With the addition of the spire in 1879, the project was complete.

The interior of the church is described as one of the finest examples of the Gothic revival in England, with its frescoes; stained glass (designed by manufacturers Clayton & Bell of Regent Street, London); delicate columns of Purbeck marble; pulpit designed by G.E. Street and carved by Dutch sculptor Thomas W. Earp; reredos, also carved by Earp, and Keble Chapel – a memorial to the Reverend John Keble, about whom more will be said shortly.

In a Service of Thanksgiving, held on 18 December 1879 to mark the completion of the transformation of the Church of St Peter, Bennett declared that the building was now capable of accommodating 1,250 persons (as opposed to 240, which was the maximum capacity of the original church). Said he, 'Our last work has been to raise the noble spire, which, by God's blessing, brings our labouring to a close'.[4] The choir sang the Te Deum and the proceedings were brought to an end with the singing of the 'Hallelujah Chorus' from Handel's oratorio *Messiah*.

Only a month later, on 19 January 1880, Bennett died. He was buried in the churchyard of St Peter's. He had been Vicar of St Peter's for almost thirty-five years.

In 1881, a memorial window for the south side of the tower was presented to the church by Bennett's two sons. Designed by G.E. Street in 1881 and known as 'The Founders

St Peter's Church. Detail from the 'Founders Window' depicting the Reverend Morden Bennett holding a model of the church.

Window', it depicts Bennett himself, together with other great church builders of history. As for the congregation, it donated, for the western transept, a 'Bennett Memorial Window' by Clayton & Bell, depicting eight scenes from the Biblical Book of Revelation.

The late Reverend A.M. Bennett also had the honour of having a brand new church built in his memory – the Anglican Church of St Stephen, designed by John Loughborough Pearson. Not only that, but the first Vicar of St Stephen's was A.S. Bennett, his son by his first marriage. St Stephen's first completed section was consecrated on 10 June 1885 by Dr Harold Browne, Bishop of Winchester.

Other churches which were established in Bournemouth included Richmond Hill Congregational (Anglican); Holy Trinity (Anglican); Punshon Memorial (Wesleyan Methodist); St Andrew's (Presbyterian) and the Oratory of the Sacred Heart (Catholic).

9

Georgina and Mary Talbot

Talbot Village in the Wallisdown area of Bournemouth, was built mainly between 1850 and 1862. This was through the generosity of two sisters; Georgina Charlotte (born 4 April 1793), and her older sister Mary Anne (born 10 April 1788), daughters of Sir George Talbot of Mickleham, Surrey.

Sir George Talbot, by now a widower, and his two daughters first visited Bournemouth in the 1840s from their London house at Grosvenor Square – exchanging the 'grey climate' of the capital for the cleaner air of the south coast. Here, Talbot purchased several properties, including Hinton Wood House on Bournemouth's East Cliff, where the family resided for part of the year. The remainder was spent either at Sir George's Mickleham Estate, or in London.

What the Talbot family encountered in Bournemouth came as something of a shock to them. Said Mary:

> All round the neighbourhood, the distress and suffering of the poor was terrible. The people used to come in crowds, calling out, 'Give us work, give us work; we are starving!' Men, women, and children came in numbers, sometimes in alarming numbers – with spades and sticks, under the windows – and the few sovereigns given away did more harm than good.[1]

There were two principal reasons for this poverty. The first was the passing, between 1760 and 1820, of the Enclosure Acts – the appropriation of common land, which had previously been available for use by the poor, as private property. The second was the Poor Law of 1834, which made it more difficult for the poor to obtain parish relief (i.e. a small, regular income, together with practical help, such as the provision of boots, and the services of a nurse in sickness from the local parish).

Sir George Talbot died on 10 June 1850, and this event gave Georgina, with her inheritance, the opportunity to act to alleviate the suffering of the poor. She was resolved, however, not simply to dispense alms (charitable donations of money or food). Instead, she would liquidate some of her assets, such as the family's Portobello Farm estates in London which she had inherited from her late father. This she did, and between 1852 and 1862, raised the sum of £150,000.

Georgina had been profoundly influenced by German author and reformer Johann Heinrich D. Zschokke (1771–1848), who extolled the virtues of religion, morality, and a concern for society's poor. In particular, it was his book *The Gold Maker's Village* which gave Georgina the notion of establishing 'Talbot Village' in Bournemouth, the building of which commenced in 1850:

> A piece of ground was hired on the Moor from Sir George Gervis, and the people were set to work under the superintendence of Mr David Tuck, the farmer; and it answered so perfectly, the people coming [from] miles and miles off [away] for work, and so grateful for the work that the whole scheme of the village gradually developed itself...[2]

Georgina Talbot. (Reproduced by permission of Bournemouth Libraries)

The land comprised 465 acres, and on it, the unemployed were set to work to build sixteen cottages – each with a garden and one acre of ground, with water well, pigsty, and fruit trees. These, they were allowed to occupy, at a rental per cottage of between £4 and £7 per annum – the idea being, that by their own industry, their occupants could now become self-sufficient. However, 'a settled rule for the village was, to have no crowding in the houses, and no lodgers permitted; and no trade carried on in the village but selling poultry, eggs, and bacon'.[3]

It was also stipulated that there was to be no public house in the village, and that if a cottager prospered sufficiently well, or came into an inheritance, then he was expected to make way for the next deserving family. There were five farms on the site which also provided employment. Finally, 150 acres of uncultivated heathland were set aside, 'for the cattle of the farms and cottages to roam over'.[4] (Georgina also acquired the Malmesbury Plantation – a pine forest later known as Talbot Woods, to which the public were allowed access).

In 1862, a school was built at Talbot Village with a house for its schoolmaster, Samuel Kerley. In the same year, a row of seven almshouses, designed by Christopher Crabbe Creeke, was opened. On its central gable were inscribed the words '*LAUS DEO*' – 'PRAISE BE TO GOD'. The almshouses were described as follows:

> The building is endowed in perpetuity for fourteen persons, with allowance of six shillings a week to each of the seven lodgments, two tons of coal, and a doctor to attend. The almshouses are intended for the old and infirm of the labouring classes not able to earn a livelihood... and here all has been done to afford peace and security to old age, and to alleviate the misery of want at the end of life.
>
> Before it lies a flower-garden and an ornamental wall, the whole open to the east and south sun, having a glorious view over the country; and behind the building is a garden for vegetables, with the means of keeping pigs and poultry for those old ones who have health and strength left to attend to those things.[5]

Further afield, in central Bournemouth, Georgina helped to finance the building of St Peter's Church (as designed by G.E. Street). She also provided more work for the poor by financing the construction of large, gabled, dwelling places in Wimborne Road, designed to accommodate the increasing number of artisans which the growing town demanded.

Finally, three acres of land were set aside for Talbot Village's Church of St Mark, to be designed by architects Evans and Fletcher, and built by Mr McWilliam at a cost of £5,000. Its foundation stone was laid by Georgina on 12 May 1868. As regards the religious instruction given therein, Georgina (said her sister Mary) was determined, 'Not to draw the cords of doctrines too tight, as to which mode of service a man might prefer; but that the foundation should be, "Love God, keep the Commandments, honour the Queen."'[6]

Talbot Village was not created without a struggle, as Mary explained:

> The outset of this village was anything but encouraging or cheerful. The first inhabitants were unused to any restraints; the women, many of them, very lax in their behaviour; the surrounding gentlemen and clergy having no sympathy with improvements or amelioration for the lower classes. [However] After a few years everything mended, but not without many troubles and vexations to the pains-taking and laborious lady [i.e. Georgina.][7]

Sadly, on 19 February 1870, shortly before the church was completed, Georgina died. The consecration of the building was then brought forward, so that she could be laid to rest in the churchyard on 9 March. Inscribed on her grave's monumental cross are the words 'GOD IS LOVE' – which is fitting, as the Christian religion was at the very core of her life. Mary now took up her late sister's mantel. She provided the church with, 'A pulpit of graceful proportions; an ancient font, procured at Rome many years ago; an organ; a complete musical service; and the furniture, in benches, chairs, &c.'[8]

Mary also had a hymnal privately printed for the congregation at her own expense, and endowed the village's day schools. She also built two more cottages. She died on 3 November 1885 at her home in Grosvenor Square. Her body was brought to Bournemouth by train, and her funeral service was held at St Mark's, where she too is buried in the churchyard.

At a service, held on 6 March 1935, to commemorate the sixty-fifth anniversary of Georgina's death, the Vicar of St Mark's, the Reverend B.R. Clutterbuck, in his sermon, told the congregation of mourners:

> If you would wish to see the memorial of the life of Miss Georgina Talbot, look around for evidence [i.e. at the village and its farms.] Her benevolence was unbounded, and her generosity of the best type.[9]

Since its opening in 1870, St Mark's Church has been enlarged, and a new church hall built. Much of Talbot Village survives and is protected by a Conservation Order which is administered by the Talbot Village Trust. The school continues to thrive as St Mark's Church of England Primary School. Of the farms, only one remains.

10

Sir Percy and Lady Shelley

Sir Percy Florence Shelley of Boscombe Manor, Bournemouth, was an interesting person, not only in his own right, but because his parents were the poet Percy Bysshe Shelley and Mary Wollstonecraft, author of the Gothic novel *Frankenstein*. Sadly, however, Sir Percy's father, the poet, died in a tragic accident when the former was only two years old.

Percy Bysshe Shelley, born on 4 August 1792, was educated at Oxford University but sent down in 1811, after circulating a pamphlet entitled 'The Necessity of Atheism'. In the same year he married Harriet Westbrook, who was aged sixteen, and by whom he had a daughter Ianthe, and a son Charles. Shelley separated from Harriet after only three years of marriage.

In July 1814, the poet eloped to France with Mary Wollstonecraft Godwin (born 30 August 1797). Mary was the daughter of philosopher, atheist, and radical free-thinker William Godwin (author of *Political Justice*) – whom Shelley admired – and his wife Mary Wollstonecraft (author of *Vindication of the Rights of Women* – which advocated the equality of the sexes and the provision of equal opportunities for women in education). In 1816, the Shelleys visited Italy and Switzerland, where, in Geneva, they met George Gordon, Lord Byron.

Sir Timothy Shelley, the poet's wealthy father, disapproved of his son's lifestyle. He refused to give the couple any assistance, and Mary therefore took up writing in an effort to make ends meet. Her most famous book, *Frankenstein*, was begun in 1816 and published in 1818. On 9 November 1816, the poet's wife Harriet committed suicide. On 30 December, only three weeks after this tragic event, he married Mary Godwin. On 12 November 1819, when the couple were living in Florence, Italy, their son Percy (the only surviving child of three) was born in Florence – hence his middle name.

On 8 July 1822, Percy's father, the poet, was drowned, aged twenty-nine, when his yacht *Ariel*, was wrecked in a gale in Greece's Bay of Spezzia. When, a few days later on 15 July, his body (and those of his two companions) was washed up on the beach at Viareggio in Italy, it was cremated on a funeral pyre in the presence of Lord Byron, James Henry Leigh Hunt (English essayist, poet and writer), and Captain Edward John Trelawney (a friend of Byron and the late Shelley). Shelley's body found its final resting place in Rome's Protestant Cemetery, but his heart, which was allegedly snatched from the flames, was brought back to England and given to his widow, Mary.

In July 1823, Mary and the three-year-old Percy returned to England, primarily in order to ensure that the latter received a good education. He attended Harrow School, and

Sir Percy Florence Shelley.

Lady Shelley.

subsequently Trinity College, Cambridge. When Charles Shelley, son of the late poet and his first wife, Harriet, died in 1826, Percy became heir to the Shelley title and estate.

On the death of his grandfather Sir Timothy Shelley in 1844, Percy inherited both the title 3rd Baronet of Castle Goring, and Sir Timothy's home 'Field Place', Horsham, Sussex. In 1845, he was admitted to the Middle Temple.

On 22 June 1848, Sir Percy married Jane (née Gibson, widow of the Honourable CR St John.) 'Field Place', however, on account of its dampness and dilapidation, was considered an unsuitable abode for both Lady Jane and Sir Percy's widowed mother Mary, neither of whom enjoyed good health. Sir Percy decided, therefore, in 1849, to purchase a house at Boscombe, a hamlet situated two miles to the east of Bournemouth, together with its 195-acre estate, where it was hoped that the two ladies would benefit from the equable climate of the region. In the event, the plans for Mary came to nought, for she died at her home at Chester Square, London, on 1 February 1851.

Prior to her death, Mary had told her daughter-in-law Lady Jane, 'I would like to rest in Bournemouth near to you, but I would like to have my father and mother with me'. Mary's wishes were granted. Her body was brought to Bournemouth and buried in a vault in the churchyard of St Peter's Church. Shortly afterwards, the remains of her parents were brought from St Pancras Churchyard, London, and re-interred with her. The Shelleys duly took up residence in Boscombe, where, having no children of their own, they adopted Jane's niece, Bessie Florence Gibson (born 1852).

The history of the Shelley's Boscombe abode is as follows. The Boscombe Estate, which included Boscombe Cottage – built at the end of the eighteenth century – was originally owned by Philip Norris. By the time Sir Percy acquired it in 1849, it had changed hands several times, had increased to 195 acres in size, and its name had been changed to Boscombe Lodge.

At Boscombe Lodge, in an alcove in Lady Shelley's boudoir called 'The Sanctum', were preserved manuscripts and relics relating to the late poet Percy Bysshe Shelley and his wife Mary. Among these artefacts was alleged to be the poet's heart. There are various legends about the fate of the poet's heart, but Lady Abinger, widow of Lady Shelley's heir, affirmed that it was placed in the Shelley tomb by Canon M.W.F. St John, Lady Shelley's nephew.[1]

In 1854, Sir Percy commissioned English sculptor Sir Henry Weekes RA, to create a monument in memory of his parents. It depicts, in white marble, a life-sized image of the drowned Shelley being cradled by his widow Mary. Beneath, on its plinth, are inscribed words from Shelley's poem 'Adonais':

> He has outsoared the shadow of our night;
> Envy and calumny and hate and pain,
> And that unrest which men miscall delight,
> Can touch him not and torture not again…

Although the monument was originally intended for St Peter's Church, Bournemouth, it was rejected by the Vicar, the Reverend A.M. Bennett, who believed that it might detract from religious worship. It was finally accepted by Christchurch Priory.

The Shelleys, both of whom were accomplished amateur actors, built a 200-seat theatre at Boscombe Lodge, complete with gallery, private box, and a bust of Sir Henry Irving, which the famous actor had presented to Lady Shelley. The theatre opened in 1856, and here the Shelleys took part in theatrical performances. In addition, Sir Percy fulfilled the roles of playwright, scene painter, and producer. The very first play – which was performed on 28 January 1856 – was a farce composed by Sir Percy entitled *He Whoops to Conquer*. Sir Percy also owned another private theatre which was adjacent to his London mansion, Shelley House, in Tite Street on the Chelsea Embankment.

Amongst the celebrated actors whom the Shelleys invited to their home, and who also acted in their plays, were Sir Henry Irving (who was a theatre manager as well as an actor) and Ellen Terry. Other guests included Robert Louis Stevenson and the poet James Henry Leigh Hunt. Boscombe Lodge now became a centre of culture and dramatic art.

The energetic Sir Percy loved sailing and was a member of the Royal Yacht Squadron. The owner of several yachts, he made a special journey by sea to the Mediterranean to visit the Gulf of Spezzia, the site of his father's tragic drowning in 1822. In 1876, Sir Percy became Commodore of the Bournemouth Regatta Club. His steam yacht *Oceana*, was the first vessel to sail from Boscombe Pier, which opened on 29 July 1889 (Sir Percy being the largest shareholder in the Boscombe Pier Company). He was also a keen cyclist and became President of the Bournemouth Bicycle and Tricycle Club.

The Shelleys participated in charitable works: one of Lady Shelley's primary interests being the restoration of the Priory Church at nearby Christchurch, in which parish Boscombe lay; they also raised money for the new Town Hall at Christchurch (built in 1859). The couple supported a proposal by Charles W. Packe of Branksome Tower to create a dispensary for the poor who had become sick, which was opened at 2 Grenville Cottages, Yelverton Road, on 15 October 1859, and which the Shelley's continued to support by holding annual fund-raising balls. In 1868, a purpose-built dispensary was opened in Stafford Road, which in 1878 was enlarged to provide fifteen beds for the sick and for victims of accidents. In 1872, the Shelleys staged a serious of amateur theatricals in aid of Bournemouth's National Sanatorium – its Annual Report for the following year indicating that Lady Shelley donated to it the sum of £300. Meanwhile, Sir Percy became one of the sanatorium's vice presidents.

In 1873, under the direction of architect Christopher Crabbe Creeke, Boscombe Lodge was virtually rebuilt, substantially enlarged, and renamed Boscombe Manor – a property which boasted its own, on-site gas works!

In 1876, the Bournemouth Amateur Dramatic Society was formed with Sir Percy as its President. In that year, he and others donated a substantial sum of money for the founding of the 'Boscombe, Pokesdown and Springbourne Provident Infirmary'. The Shelleys also supported Bournemouth's British School in Orchard Street, which Sir Percy believed should 'be run on broad and liberal lines without any reference to party or religious denominations'.[2] It opened in 1879.

Sir Percy Florence Shelley died on 5 December 1889 aged seventy years, and was buried in the family vault at St Peter's. There being no children, the baronetcy passed to Sir Percy's cousin, Edward Shelley. Lady Shelley died a decade later on 24 June 1899 aged seventy-nine years; she was also buried in the family vault.

Bearing in mind the non-conforming attitude of both his parents, it is hardly surprising that Percy Bysshe Shelley, the poet, became something of a rebel. His son, Sir Percy, however, steadied the ship. He became a highly respected pillar of society, and with his wife Lady Shelley, performed many good deeds and added colour by attracting many of the foremost artists of the day – including poets and writers, as well as actors – to his Bournemouth home and theatre.

Following Lady Shelley's death in 1899, Boscombe Manor was inherited by her great-nephew Shelley Leopold Lawrence Scarlett (who in 1903 became the 5th Baron Abinger). To Bournemouth Corporation, Scarlett donated six acres of land on the cliffs at Boscombe, in perpetuity, with the result that Boscombe Cliff Gardens were opened to the public on 6 June 1900 in the presence of the Mayor and Corporation.

Sir Percy would have been gratified to know that on 27 May 1895, six years after his death, Boscombe's own Grand Pavilion Theatre (later known as Boscombe Theatre, and finally as the Boscombe Hippodrome), designed by Messrs Lawson and Donkin with seats for 3,000 people, was opened at a cost of £16,000.

In 1911, Boscombe Manor was purchased by the Bournemouth Beach Committee. It subsequently became, for a time, the Grovely Manor School for girls, and later still as 'Shelley Manor', the home of the Poole and Bournemouth College of Art and Design. Recently, thanks to the fund-raising activities of the 'Friends of Shelley Manor', a local residents action group, the Shelley Theatre (a Grade II listed building) and library are to be restored, and the defunct Shelley Museum recreated. The remainder of the property will serve as flats, residential apartments, and a doctors' surgery.

11

Christopher Crabbe Creeke

Of all the interesting characters who played a part in shaping the new town of Bournemouth, none was more creative than Christopher Creeke, who arrived there in the year 1852.

Creeke was born on 11 March 1820 at Cambridge, where he received his education. He became a pupil of the celebrated London architect Sir Sidney Smirk, and subsequently joined the firm of London land surveyor Henry Lee. In 1845, he married Elizabeth Norwood. He was a founder member of the Architectural Association, founded in 1847, and the following year he became its President (until 1850). In 1852, when Creeke moved to Bournemouth, he went into partnership with A.H. Parken. His first home was Windsor Cottage on Richmond Hill.

On 14 July 1856, 'The Bournemouth Improvement Act' received its Royal Assent. This was 'An Act for the Improvement of Part of the District of St Peter Bournemouth in the Parishes of Christchurch and Holdenhurst in the County of Southampton, and for Providing a Pier there'. Thirteen Commissioners were appointed whose task it was to see that the provisions of the Act were implemented. As for Creeke, he himself was appointed 'Surveyor and Inspector of Nuisances' to the Commissioners, for which he was paid the modest sum of £50 per annum. In this capacity, Creeke's task was:

… to advise, report on and prepare estimates for any works from time to time contemplated by the commissioners relating to the profession, and to provide all the requisite plans, specifications and superintendence of work…

A considerable part of Mr Creeke's early years under the Commissioners was devoted to levelling the surface of the roads – lowering here, raising there – gravelling, channelling, and curbing; all spare soil being thrown over the cliff. The first road to be attended to was Westover Road, described as, 'the principle residential quarter,' where six labourers were employed laying down gravel and shaping and curbing the roadway.[1]

According to the Bournemouth Guardian of 6 February 1909:

Wherever the Bournemouth man comes across, in the old town, winding roads, roads with strips of bushes between the carriage way and the paths, roads with oases of trees where they met other road curves and bends, and an absence of right angles and stiffness, there he will see the mark of Christopher Crabbe Creeke.

Christopher Crabbe Creeke by W.J.Warren, 1888. (Reproduced with the kind permission of Russell-Cotes Art Gallery and Museum)

Bournemouth in 1855, with Belle Vue Hotel, Library ('Reading Room'), Baths, and first Jetty. (Reproduced by permission of Bournemouth Libraries)

Creeke relocated to Lainston Villa, Exeter Lane, which is where he based his architectural practice. This is also where the Bournemouth Commissioners held their meetings between 1858 and 1874, when the first Town Hall was built. Creeke's:

> … duties were incredibly varied and thoroughly complicated. He was armed with powers to construct roads, sewers and drains, to pave, light, cleanse, drain water, and improve public thoroughfares, and to remove and prevent nuisances and encroachments… Parallel with this work, Mr Creeke was busy with the water-supply and sanitation.
>
> This amazing man, tireless and enthusiastic in his town's welfare, also drained swampy meadows, which are now the Lower Pleasure Gardens enjoyed by so many. First attempts at lighting the town's thoroughfares were inaugurated by the ebullient Mr Creeke.[2]

In early 1859, the Commissioners engaged engineer George Rennie (son of Scottish engineer John Rennie) to design a wooden pier. Rennie's plans were speedily approved, and on 25 July, work was commenced. The pier was duly opened by Sir George Tapps Gervis on 17 September 1861 with a celebratory procession, firework display, and twenty-one-gun salute. Whereupon, 'the British flag was unfurled', and a band played the national anthem.[3] The pier, however, was unable to withstand the combined assaults of shipworm beetle and heavy storms; so that by 1876, it had become so badly damaged as to be unfit to receive steamer traffic. It was replaced by a new iron pier in 1880.

As an entry in the *Bournemouth Visitors Directory* for 26 May 1886 indicates, Creeke 'was particularly fond of the classical style of architecture and may be said to have inaugurated the detached villa system which has proved so unique a characteristic of the town'. In summary, Creeke's avowed aim was to create 'steady development, with judicious tree-planting and no overcrowding'.[4]

He was also employed as Surveyor and Agent to the Clapcott Dean Estate (in which capacity he prepared plans for Dean Park and for the West Cliff estates), the Durrant Estate (which he planned and laid out), and the Stourcliff Estate.

In 1879, Creeke retired, whereupon the Bournemouth Commissioners appointed him consulting engineer at a salary of £200 per annum. In 1883, he was rewarded by being elected a Commissioner himself. In that year, he formed a new partnership with Charles Gifford, his former pupil and chief assistant.

The number of projects with which Creeke became involved was truly prodigious. As architect, he designed the following:

- The Belle Vue Assembly Rooms (mid-1850s), situated at the rear of the Belle View Hotel, which served 'for a multitude of purposes, all [musical] concerts, and meetings of a public character being held there'. This was also where the Bournemouth Commissioners held their meetings from 1856–57

- Richmond Hill Congregational Church (1859, replaced in 1891)

- The almshouses at Talbot Village (1862)

Perambulations in the pines, *c.* 1870. (Fraser Donachie)

- Holy Trinity Church (1869, with architect A.H. Park)

- Hume Towers, Branksome Wood Road (1871 – home of Sir Joshua Walmsley)

- the first Town Hall (it should be mentioned that in 1887, the Theatre Royal, Albert Road, was converted into Bournemouth's second Town Hall. When the Town Hall transferred to Yelverton Road in 1892, the building reverted to being a theatre. Finally, in 1921, the Hotel Mont Dore became the present-day Town Hall)

- Boscombe Place (Manor – reconstruction and enlargement for Sir Percy Shelley, 1873)

- the chapels of Bournemouth's Wimborne Road Cemetery (1877, whose grounds he also laid out)

- the Wilts and Dorset Bank (established in Bournemouth in 1861, with premises in Old Christchurch Road, which were designed by Creeke and opened in 1878)

- the Hahnemann Convalescent Home and Dispensary (1879, built on the West Cliff and named after German physician Dr Christian Friedrich Samuel Hahnemann, who founded the art of homeopathy)

- the Royal Bath Hotel (addition of two new wings, for Sir Merton Russell-Cotes, 1880)

- the Shaftesbury Hall and Gymnasium in St Peter's Road (erected as a memorial to the late Earl of Shaftesbury, to be used for public meetings, concerts, etc)

- the Wilberforce Coffee Tavern (Holdenhurst Road)

- and the Baptist Chapel (Lansdowne)

When Bournemouth's Dispensary was deemed to be inadequate, it fell to Messrs Creeke and Gifford to design a new hospital – the foundation stone of which was laid on 21 June 1887 (the year after Creeke's death) in recognition of Queen Victoria's Golden Jubilee. Named the Royal Victoria Hospital and situated in Poole Road, Westbourne, it was opened on 16 January 1890 by the Prince of Wales (later King Edward VII).

Further afield, Creeke laid out: the Branksome Tower Estate, Poole (1852 – designed by architect W. Burn of London for Charles W. Packe MP, one of Bournemouth's commissioners); a memorial monument in London to Daniel Defoe, and Union workhouses at Christchurch, Blandford, Tisbury and Chippenham. As if this were not enough to occupy him, Creeke served as commandant of the 19th Hants Rifle Volunteers 'for upwards of 20 years, and when he retired he was permitted to retain his honorary rank [of captain], and was always delighted to turn up at the annual presentations of prizes and on other occasions in uniform'.[5]

Creeke died on 22 May 1886 at the age of sixty-six at his home, which was now Dean Hurst, Dean Park. He was buried at Bournemouth's Wimborne Road Cemetery, the chapel of which he had designed himself (as architect and surveyor to the Burial Board).

12

Charles Lavington Pannel

Pannel, son of John Pannel, a clergyman, was born on 23 January 1818. A resident of Guildford, Surrey, he may justly be regarded as the founder of Bournemouth's National Sanatorium for Consumption and Diseases of the Chest. His wife, Catherine Louisa (née Hugonin) of Buriton near Petersfield in Hampshire, whom he married on 23 May 1848, was the daughter of an Army colonel. When he married Catherine he was described as a widower living in London, with the occupation of gamekeeper.

In the year 1854, German botanist Dr Hermann Brehmer (1826-89) opened the world's first sanatorium for tuberculosis in the mountains at Gorbersdorf in the Prussian province of Silesia. Here, the 'open-air' method of treatment was used, about which more will be said shortly.

Three years prior to this, on 11 December 1851, the Management Committee of London's Brompton Hospital (founded in 1841 and originally called The Hospital for Consumption and Diseases of the Chest, of which Pannel was Treasurer and Honorary Secretary), made an announcement in *The Times* newspaper to the effect that it intended to create a convalescent home for 'destitute patients' who were recovering from, or were in the early stages of, consumption. In his Report for 1854, Pannel explained how this had come about. Medical Officers of the Brompton Hospital had observed '… that in many cases, the progress of consumptive disease can be arrested, and health so far restored, as to enable the individual to leave hospital comparatively well'. Unhappily, however, many patients who were sent home:

> … before their health is fully established… [as a result were] often driven by their necessities to engage in various unhealthy occupations… [which rendered them liable] to suffer from a recurrence of the disease. [Therefore] with the object of counteracting this great evil, it was proposed by some friends of the [Brompton] Hospital for Consumption, to establish an independent Institution in a suitable situation on the Southern Coast of England, to which patients requiring change of air and climate might be sent.

Having considered several sites on the south coast, the committee of the Brompton finally chose Bournemouth, a place which possessed, 'in a high degree, the three great requisites of a healthy situation – dryness, equability, and mildness of temperature.'

Pannel now provided further details of how such a sanatorium was to be run. It would be managed by a committee of the Brompton, assisted by a local committee based in

Bournemouth, and staffed by a resident medical officer and a matron. Like its parent hospital in London, Bournemouth's 'National Sanatorium' was to be a voluntary hospital, meaning that it relied on donations from members of the public and wealthy members of society to fund its activities:

> Donors of thirty guineas and upwards become Governors for life; and Subscribers of three guineas will be Governors during the continuance of their subscription. A Subscriber of one guinea will have the privilege of recommending one patient [for admission to the sanatorium] every third year.

It was envisaged that patients might have to remain in Bournemouth for a considerable time – the entire winter, for example – in order that they might derive a 'permanent advantage from the climate…'. As the income from subscriptions would be insufficient to meet the expense of such prolonged residence, 'it has been determined that every patient shall contribute three shillings and sixpence per week towards his or her maintenance…'.[1]

The National Sanatorium, designed by architect Edward Buckton Lamb and built on land provided by George Durrant, Esq., cost in the order of £15,000. It opened on Monday 1 October 1855, providing beds for fifteen male and fifteen female patients, and was staffed by a (non-resident) physician, matron, cook, kitchen maid and porter. However, from 1856, beds were provided for a number of 'guinea patients' who paid one guinea per week, and who were housed in the sanatorium's upper corridor. In those days, before the infectious nature of tuberculosis was recognized, patients who were well enough were permitted to venture into the town. In fact, a favourite route taken by them through the wood adjoining the Lower Gardens, became known as 'Invalids Walk' (and subsequently, Pine Walk).

In May 1857, the connection with the Brompton Hospital ceased by mutual consent, and sole responsibility for the National Sanatorium passed to Pannel, who, in order to ensure that it continued to flourish, proceeded to enlist the patronage of the wealthy and the titled. For example, vice patrons of the sanatorium included three earls and a lord; its president was the Bishop of Winchester.

In 1863, a new East Wing – designed by Christopher Crabbe Creeke – provided accommodation for an additional twelve patients, who arrived at the sanatorium from all over England, and also from Wales and Scotland. In 1864, no less than forty occupations were listed, including that of blacksmith, clergyman, doctor, governess, labourer, Army officer, policeman, schoolmistress, schoolboy, schoolgirl and victualler. In that year, the sanatorium building and grounds were vested in the hands of trustees, one of whom was Pannel, and its management was entrusted to a committee of twenty-four members. On 6 June 1865, the foundation stone of the sanatorium's Chapel of St Luke – the 'good physician' and gospel writer – designed by G.E. Street, was laid by C.W. Packe, Esq. MP of Branksome Tower. It opened for Divine Service on 18 October 1866 – St Luke's Day.

Despite Pannel's best efforts, the sanatorium was always short of money, to the extent that on 28 October 1868, the following advertisement appeared in *The Times* newspaper:

BOURNEMOUTH, ROYAL NATIONAL SANATORIUM SOUTH FRONT.

Bournemouth's Royal National Sanatorium for Consumption and Diseases of the Chest, South Front. (Royal Bournemouth Hospital Library)

The Committee regret to say that a deficiency of £674 will make it necessary to close one of the wards this winter, unless further funds are immediately forthcoming.

This appeal – and others like it – was successful, for in 1870, a new West Wing (designed by Bromfield of London) was opened in stages, to provide twenty additional beds, two dining halls and servants' quarters. In order to raise funds, a bazaar was held at the sanatorium. Further fund-raising bazaars were held, both at the sanatorium and at Brownsea Castle – on Brownsea Island in Poole Harbour.

Pannel now proposed that the establishment close each summer – during July and August – on account of the hot weather, during which time its wards could be cleansed by washing down with a solution of lime. In that year, the first resident medical officer was appointed. From 1874, 'guinea patients' were no longer admitted, and the sanatorium was given over entirely to poor patients, as was originally intended.

Other institutions in Bournemouth which catered for tubercular patients included: the St Mary's Home for Invalid Ladies in Dean Park Road, established in 1871, which provided 'a home of rest' for ten ladies 'with limited means who are in the early or curable stages of consumption...'[2] and the Hahnemann Convalescent Home and Homoeopathic Dispensary, which opened on the West Cliff on 3 June 1879.

1885 saw the opening of the Hotel Mont Dore, which was situated immediately adjacent to the sanatorium. Residents of the hotel were invited to use the sanatorium's chapel, and in 1887, it was proposed that the two buildings be linked by a covered way, to enable residents of the hotel to attend services without having to venture outdoors. As a *quid pro quo*, the

Mont Dore's baths were put at the disposal of the patients in the sanatorium. Had it been known at the time that tuberculosis was an infectious disease, this would not have been allowed to happen, for instead of eradicating tuberculosis, the National Sanatorium was actually encouraging its spread!

Non-tubercular patients were also catered for at the sanatorium. In 1886, for example, twenty-one chronic bronchitics, and twenty with heart disease and 'anaemia with delicate lungs' were admitted and treated.[3] In 1888, a new South-West Wing was added, together with winter garden and covered tennis court. In that year, Pannel resigned as treasurer and became one of its vice presidents. Throughout his lifetime he had also continued to support the Brompton Hospital with gifts of money.

In 1898-99, the open-air method of treatment, as had been practised by Brehmer from 1854 onwards, was adopted by most sanatoria in Britain. This included Bournemouth's National Sanatorium, where sleeping huts and day shelters were constructed in the grounds. Men and women were segregated, and the men's section included a croquet lawn. The adoption by the sanatorium of this new regime annoyed the residents of the Hotel Mont Dore, who could hear the constant coughing of the patients from their rooms. They would have been even more annoyed, if not horrified, had they known that they were also being exposed to airborne droplets which were likely to infect them with tuberculosis! In that year, Pannel contributed the sum of £500 to the sanatorium's funds.[4]

The Royal National Sanatorium (area reserved for men). (Royal Bournemouth Hospital Library)

The Royal National Sanatorium – area reserved for women. (Royal Bournemouth Hospital Library)

The Royal National Sanatorium staff with Dr Snow and Matron Todd, *c.* 1900. (Royal Bournemouth Hospital Library)

The Royal National Sanatorium staff with Matron Lloyd, *c.* 1909. (Royal Bournemouth Hospital Library)

Pannel died on 10 April 1905 aged eighty-seven years, having spent the last decade of his life at Ryde on the Isle of Wight. Following his death, a ward at the National Sanatorium was named after him.[5] In that same year, the sanatorium was granted the title 'Royal'. Pannel's wife Catherine, died on 7 May 1908. Both are buried in Ryde Cemetery.

Pannel's portrait, allegedly, once hung in the reception room of the National Sanatorium. Sadly, its present whereabouts is unknown.

W.H. Smith and Family

W.H. Smith (I) of London, son of the founder of British retailer W.H. Smith & Son, lived in Bournemouth from 1859 to 1865, which were the last six years of his life. His father was Henry Walton Smith, born in 1738 of a well-to-do family from Hinton St George in Somerset, whose background was as follows.

In the 1780s, Henry moved to London, where he became assistant to Charles Rogers, Customs Officer of the London Custom House. On 27 October 1784 he married Anna Eastaugh, a domestic servant twenty years his junior, whereupon he was promptly disowned by his family. Despite this setback, Henry established a 'news-walk' (paper round) and newspaper-vending business, which he conducted in London's fashionable district of Mayfair. He and Anna had three children: Henry Edward (1787), Mary Anne (1789), and William Henry (W.H. Smith I), who was born on 15 July 1792.

Henry died on 23 August 1792, the month after his youngest son was born. Subsequently, Anna not only kept the business alive, but in 1815, she expanded it by acquiring a nearby booksellers, newsagents and stationers. When she died the following year, the business was divided between her two sons, and became 'H & W Smith'.

In 1817, W.H. Smith (I) married Mary Anne Cooper, who bore him six (surviving) daughters and a son, William Henry Smith (II), who was born on 24 June 1825. In 1828, W.H. Smith I's brother Henry left the company, which then became simply 'W.H. Smith'. In 1846, when W.H. Smith (II) attained his majority, he became his father's junior partner, and the business now became 'W.H. Smith & Son'.

In 1848, taking advantage of the current boom in railway travel, the firm began to open bookstalls and newspaper vending facilities on railway stations. It also made use of the railways to become the country's leading distributor of national newspapers. As a result, the business went from strength to strength.

For some time, members of the Smith family had expressed concern about the way W.H. Smith (I) was driving himself. For example, in an undated letter to W.H. Smith (II), the latter's sister, Emma, indicated just how anxious she was about her workaholic father '…I am sorry dear Father is so extremely diligent in business, but the time will come when in some way our God will answer our earnest and united prayers…'[1]

Likewise, on 28 October 1845, W.H. Smith (II) had written to another of his sisters, Mary Anne, to say that, 'He [WH Smith (I)] had felt the pressure of the business – had been worried by it and had suffered in his nerves…'. He also told Mary Anne that his father 'had at last made up his mind to retire as soon as he could possibly get things in order'.[2]

W.H. Smith (I).
(W.H. Smith Archives)

Walton House in the early 1920s. (W.H. Smith Archives)

However, by 17 March 1851, the date on which W.H. Smith (I)'s wife Mary died, he had still not retired. Mary was buried in London's Kensal Green Cemetery.

In 1857, W.H. Smith (I) did finally retire, whereupon his son, W.H. Smith (II), assumed full control of the company. Two years later, the former moved to Bournemouth to live with his unmarried daughter Anna Augusta Smith, at Walton House, Richmond Hill, a large villa set in an acre of ground and overlooking the sea; built by himself and named after his father, Henry Walton Smith.

In Bournemouth, W.H. Smith (I) became a governor of the National Sanatorium, and one of its most generous benefactors. Here, he received visits from the family, including his son W.H. Smith (II), who on 13 April 1858 had married widow Emily Leach, daughter of Frederick Dawes Danvers, formerly Clerk to the Council of the Duchy of Lancaster.

It was with some consternation that W.H. Smith (I) received news, in 1860, that his son W.H. Smith (II) intended to stand for Parliament. His response was as follows, 'Anything that takes you so much from Emily would be a severe trouble to her'. He was also anxious about the possible detrimental effect on W.H. Smith & Son. Said he, 'It will be little worse than Insanity for you to adopt a course that would occupy time to such an extent that the business must be neglected'.[3]

On a more mundane level, W.H. Smith (I) was also concerned that here in Bournemouth, his daily newspapers were not being delivered in accordance with his wishes. 'I really hope my old business is not conducted in this neglectful and blundering way', he exclaimed.[4]

W.H. Smith (I) died at his Bournemouth home on 28 July 1865. He too is buried at Kensal Green Cemetery. He is commemorated in the chapel of the National Sanatorium by a window, a reredos, and a plaque; all provided by Anna. The three-light, stained-glass tracery window by Clayton & Bell depicts the Resurrection and Ascension of Christ, with words from the Holy Bible's New Testament, 'I go to prepare a place for you', and 'I am the resurrection and the life'.[5] The stone reredos was carved by G.E. Street's favourite sculptor Thomas W. Earp, its subject being the Good Samaritan. On the brass plaque are inscribed the words:

> In memory of William Henry Smith of Walton House,
> A Life Governor of the Hospital, who died July 28th, 1865, aged 73 years.
> The eastern window is placed in the chapel by his daughter Anna Augusta.

Anna died in 1889 in Torquay. In her will, she left £300 to the National Sanatorium.

W.H. Smith (II) ignored his late father's advice, and having entered Parliament in 1868, became one of Queen Victoria's most respected ministers, rising, by the year 1887, to be Leader of the House of Commons. He too took a lively interest in charitable work, and like his late father, was a governor of London's King's College Hospital. He also supported Bournemouth's National Sanatorium, becoming a member of its committee – a post from which he resigned in 1888 when he was appointed one of its vice presidents. One of the sanatorium's principal benefactors, he donated the sum of £697 10s 0d to that organization during his lifetime.[6] He also lent his name to a national campaign to raise funds for the sanatorium.

The National Sanatorium – Chapel
of St Luke the Physician. (Royal
Bournemouth Hospital Library)

W.H. Smith (I) memorial window.
(Brompton Court Management)

W.H. Smith (I) memorial reredos. (Brompton Court Management)

W.H. Smith (II) died on 6 October 1891 aged sixty-six, at Walmer Castle, Kent, which was his official residence (as holder of the position of Lord Warden of the Cinque Ports). In his will he left £1,000 to the sanatorium. When, in his honour, Queen Victoria made his widow Emily a peeress, she took the title of Viscountess Hambleden.

Emily had borne W.H. Smith (II) four daughters and one (surviving) son, the Honourable William Frederick Danvers Smith, born on 12 August 1868. On the death of his father in 1891, W.F.D. Smith, now aged twenty-three, entered the business and two years later became its head. He also continued the family's association with Bournemouth's National Sanatorium, whose Committee of Management he joined. He also featured on its subscription list, and in 1906 became its treasurer.

On his mother's death in 1913, W.F.D. Smith (who resided at 'Greenlands', Hambleden, Henley-on-Thames, Oxfordshire, but retained his late mother's home in Bournemouth) inherited the title Lord Hambleden. In 1925, he became the sanatorium's third president. He died in 1928, and in that year, W.H. Smith & Son was reconstituted as a limited company.

Another of W.H. Smith (II's) sisters, Priscilla, born in 1833, married the Reverend John Henry Phillips of Okeford Fitzpaine, Dorset. She bore him four children – the youngest being Charles Augustine Phillips, who followed in his father's footsteps and became a clergyman.

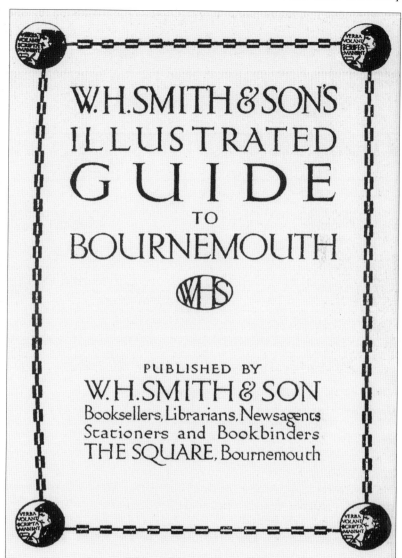

W.H. Smith's
*Illustrated Guide
to Bournemouth,*
published 1919.

In 1943, the Reverend C.A. Phillips, who for the past eight years had been Licensed Priest for the Diocese of Winchester, became Chaplain to Bournemouth Royal National Sanatorium. In the same year, he was appointed Assistant Curate of the town's Holy Trinity Church, a position which he held until his death in 1950. Here, tuberculous patients were permitted to worship, but only in a designated area enclosed by a glass screen.[7] Canon Frederick Bussby, who wrote the history of Holy Trinity Church, described Phillips as its 'most scholarly priest';[8] an indication of his scholarliness being demonstrated in the letters which he wrote from Bournemouth to English biblical scholar and curator of manuscripts, James Rendel Harris. These letters contain accounts of the Reverend Phillips's '… research on the background to the gospels, and visits to the British Museum and other libraries.

Wedding of Helena Agnes Phillips to Professor M. Laurie, 29 December 1898. From left to right, back row: Reverend Charles Augustine Phillips (bride's brother); Professor A.P. Laurie (groom's brother); unknown Bridesmaid; Helena Agnes Phillips (bride); Professor M. Laurie (groom); Reverend Frank Benet Phillips (bride's brother) and his wife Eleanor Fanny (née Hanson-Smith). Front row: Reverend John Henry Phillips and his wife Priscilla (née Smith), the bride's parents; Clara Elizabeth Phillips (bride); unknown; Professor S.S. Laurie, father of the groom.

He also writes about some research in Europe, and uses his knowledge of Syriac and the classical languages to make constructive comparisons between the New Testament and other literature of the period'.[9]

Holy Trinity's 'Phillips Memorial Library' was named after the Reverend Phillips. Sadly, the church was destroyed by fire in 1981.

14

Others associated with the National Sanatorium

A brief account is given of some other people who were involved with the National Sanatorium in its early years:

When Bournemouth was chosen by the Brompton Hospital Committee as the most suitable location on which to build the National Sanatorium, local landowner George Durrant Esq. of Norwich, owner of Bournemouth's Branksome Estate, offered, in early 1853, a three-acre plot of land for the purpose.[1]

Dr Edward Vincent Mainwaring was the only member of the town's National Sanatorium Committee who resided in Bournemouth, all the other members lived in London or the Home Counties. Mainwaring, who was Bournemouth's first resident doctor, also assisted the sanatorium by donating to it the proceeds from a course of lectures which he gave on anatomy in the school hall of St Peter's Church.

Sir George Tapps Gervis was one of the sanatorium's six vice presidents. He also featured on its Subscription List.

On 10 July 1855, an amateur theatrical performance of William Wilkie Collins's play *The Lighthouse,* was staged by English writer Charles Dickens in aid of the Bournemouth National Sanatorium. The play, produced at Colonel Waugh's miniature theatre at Campden House, Kensington, is set in Plymouth's Eddystone Lighthouse in the year 1748. Dickens, a friend of Collins, played the part of the head lightkeeper Aaron Gurnock, and Collins himself played the part of Gurnock's son, Martin. Dickens was also a regular subscriber to the Brompton Hospital.

The Reverend A.M. Bennett, Rector of St Peter's Church, was a staunch supporter of the sanatorium, raising money for it by means of his 'subscription lists', and also by holding regular collections at St Peter's. He also served, from 1864 to 1869, as the sanatorium's chaplain.

Edward Buckton Lamb was the architect chosen to design the sanatorium (which cost the sum of £3,100). This he did, in the Italianate style. The building contractor is believed to have been John Score and his son Samuel, from Wimborne.[2] Lamb also designed Branksome Dene, bordering on Alum Chine – the home of C.A. King.

Dr Willoughby Marshall Burslem MD, FRCP, was the sanatorium's first physician. Born in 1819, he was highly experienced in the treatment of consumption, having worked, amongst other places, at the Brompton Hospital. His book, *Pulmonary Consumption and its Treatment*, was published in 1852. Upon retiring in 1870, he was appointed Consultant Physician to the sanatorium. When he died in 1889, a ward was named after him.

Dr W.W. Humby was the sanatorium's first resident medical officer, from 1870 to 1886.

The Reverend James Hibbert Wanklyn was the sanatorium's first chaplain, in which capacity he served from 1855 to 1864, and from 1872 to 1875. Prayers and services were held regularly throughout the week at the sanatorium's chapel, attendance at which was compulsory. In 1861, Wanklyn purchased the site immediately to the east of the sanatorium, where he built his house, 'The Glen'. Here, he held fund-raising concerts in aid of the sanatorium.

The Reverend Oldfield K. Prescott succeeded Wanklyn as chaplain in 1876, in which capacity he served for thirty-one years. He also served as member of the Management Committee for thirty-eight years.

George Matlock was the sanatorium's porter. One of his five children died of tuberculosis.

Christopher Crabbe Creeke designed the sanatorium's East End Extension which opened in 1863, providing accommodation for twelve additional patients together with staffrooms.

George Edmund Street of London, designed the sanatorium's Chapel of St Luke the Physician, which was completed in 1866. As already mentioned, he was also the designer of Bournemouth's second, modified and enlarged St Peter's Church. The finance for the building of the chapel was largely provided by the Reverend A.M. Bennett through his 'subscription list'.

In 1869, Queen Victoria became patron of the sanatorium.

In 1870, Dr William Stewart Falls succeeded Dr Burslem as physician to the sanatorium, in which capacity he served until 1887. When he died, two years later, a ward was named after him, in accordance with tradition.

It was the Reverend S.R. Waddelow's idea to found Firs Bank in Old Christchurch Road, 'an institution primarily intended for consumptives whose cure at the sanatorium is despaired of'. It opened in 1872.[3]

In the 1870s, Sir Percy Florence Shelley became one of the sanatorium's vice presidents. In 1873, he raised the sum of £380 from theatrical performances held at his home, Boscombe Manor, in aid of the sanatorium's new West Wing.[4] His wife Lady Shelley, was a governor of the Brompton Hospital.

Sir Henry Taylor presented the sanatorium with the sum of £500, to be designated as 'Aubrey's Gift' – in memory of the late Irish poet Aubrey de Vere (1788-1846), a friend of his and a cousin of his wife, Theodosia. Under the terms of the gift, it was stipulated that 'the incumbent or Vicar of St Peter's Church, Bournemouth, shall be authorized to nominate one, poor, male inmate of the Sanatorium who shall be discharged from [i.e. absolved from] the weekly payment of six shillings'.

Nurse Pigrome appears in the 1881 records as the first trained nurse to be mentioned as being an employee of the sanatorium.

Dan Godfrey founded the Bournemouth Musical Orchestra (the first of a permanent nature to be established in the country) in 1893, and was its leading conductor until 1934. He and his musicians frequently visited the sanatorium and entertained the residents with musical concerts. In 1922 he received a knighthood.

On Queen Victoria's death in 1901, she was succeeded by her son, King Edward VII, as patron of the sanatorium. In 1902, the King donated the sum of £100 to the sanatorium. He, in turn, was succeeded, successively, as patron by King George V and Queen Mary, the Duke of York, Queen Mary, and Princess Margaret.

Did the National Sanatorium benefit its patients? In many ways, yes, in that they were given shelter and medical attention, and in the case of the poor, relieved of the necessity of having to earn their living. They also benefited from the good food provided (which included eggs, bacon, sausages, fish, mutton, beef, sago, rice pudding and porridge),[5] and, of course, from the congenial atmosphere of Bournemouth.

As for the medical treatment offered, whereas the motivation, industry, and dedication of the staff cannot be impugned, it is likely that this was of only marginal benefit. It was only when the antibiotic streptomycin became available in Britain from 1948 onwards, that the prospect of a cure for the disease became a possibility. Also, at a time when tuberculosis was not generally recognized as an infectious disease, it has to be admitted that the sanatorium, by allowing its patients to: venture into the town; by placing its chapel at the disposal of residents at the adjacent Hotel Mont Dore; by allowing its patients use of the Mont Dore's baths, and by allowing the families of certain members of staff – such as porter, George Matlock – to live on the premises, was actually encouraging the spread of the disease.

On 29 September 1902, the Charity Organization Society of The Strand, London, announced in *The Times* that 'the Royal National Hospital at Ventnor [Isle of Wight] and the National Sanatorium at Bournemouth are often so full that admission to them cannot be obtained unless after a delay of from 12 to 16 weeks…'

It was to be another nine years before this serious state of affairs was put right, by the Insurance Act of 1911. Proposed by David Lloyd George, Chancellor of the Exchequer in H.H. Asquith's Liberal government, the Act made it a legal requirement for local authorities to provide dispensaries where out-patients suffering from tuberculosis could be treated. A dispensary was therefore built in the grounds of the Royal National Sanatorium for this purpose, and staffed for two and a half days of the week by its resident medical officer.[6] In addition, each local authority was obliged to reserve sanatoria beds for advanced cases who were beyond recovery, and to this end, sixteen beds at the sanatorium were reserved for the purpose, with another four beds being reserved at The Firs home. Also, under the Act, working class people became eligible for sickness benefits. They were now able to pay for their treatment at sanatoria without having to depend on sponsorship.

During the First World War, twenty of the sanatorium's beds were allocated for service personnel with tuberculosis – they included some Belgians and two New Zealanders. In 1930, x-ray equipment was installed. During the Second World War, the sanatorium treated about twenty servicemen per year. On 24 May 1942, the chapel was slightly damaged by an enemy bomb which fell on the Pleasure Gardens. In 1948, the sanatorium ceased to be a voluntarily-maintained enterprise, when it was taken over by the management of the South West Metropolitan Regional Hospital Board and became the responsibility of the state.

In 1950, Bournemouth contained in excess of 400 sanatoria beds, including those of the Royal National Sanatorium, Douglas House (for ex-servicemen), The Firs, the Herbert Hospital, Linford Sanatorium, Highcliffe Children's Home and Christchurch Hospital (twelve beds). When the sanatorium was founded in 1855, the death rate from pulmonary tuberculosis in England and Wales was 27.7 per 10,000 living. By 1953, it had fallen to 1.79 per 10,000 living.

In 1966, a new out-patient chest clinic was opened in the grounds of the sanatorium, which now became the Royal National Hospital. In 1989, the Royal National Hospital closed with the opening of the Royal Bournemouth Hospital, Castle Lane East. As for the sanatorium, it was converted – in the year 2000 – into Brompton Court, to provide sheltered accommodation for the elderly. The chapel has been preserved.

15

Sir Henry and Lady Taylor

Civil servant, poet and writer, Sir Henry Taylor acquired a house in Bournemouth in late 1861, which he and his wife Theodosia and family used as a summer residence, and to which he subsequently retired.

Sir Henry, son of Mr George Taylor of Witton Hall, Durham, was born on 18 October 1800 at Bishop-Middleham in that county. In April 1814, he entered the Royal Navy as midshipman, but made only one sea voyage and was discharged in December on the grounds of ill health.

In 1816, Sir Henry came to London. Having paid a visit to the Windward Islands, he returned home and began to contribute articles to the *Quarterly Review* – the most influential periodical of the time. In 1823, he became editor of the *London Magazine* (covering literature and the arts). In January 1824, he was appointed clerk in the Colonial Office. In 1839, he married Theodosia Alicia Ellen Charlotte Spring-Rice, daughter of Lord Monteagle of Brandon. In 1853, he and his family made their home at Sheen in Derbyshire. During his long career, Sir Henry served under no less than twenty-six Secretaries of State; he also found time for poetry and literature.

Sir Henry wrote several plays, the most notable being *Philip van Artevelde* (1834), a historic drama in blank verse, set in the Flemish town of Ghent in the fourteenth century, and commemorating the life of the Flemish patriot of that name. The play was staged in 1847, but ran for only six nights. He also wrote a satirical essay, *The Statesman* (1836), on the art of succeeding as a civil servant. A friend of poets Byron, Wordsworth, Coleridge, Southey, Rogers, and other literati of the day, Sir Henry's own collection of lyrical poems was published in 1845.

Sir Henry first came to Bournemouth in 1861, to spend two months of the summer with his family. Said he:

> This place is beautiful beyond any seaside place I have ever seen except the Riviera, and the air is dry and pure, unacquainted with anything but the sea, the pine woods which reach for miles inland, and the sandy soil in which they grow. It is a place where nature is the holiday-maker, and man is at rest...

The fine quality of Bournemouth's air was of particular interest to Sir Henry, who, as an asthma sufferer, had been obliged to work from home since 1859. By the December of 1861, he had '... found a house half built, which we bought and finished to our taste.

Sir Henry Taylor.

Lady Taylor.

We are to live in it in the summer and let it in the winter'. The house to which Sir Henry referred, named 'The Roost', was situated in Church Road (subsequently renamed Hinton Road). However, he complained about the local residents, who consisted of '… two clergymen [the Reverend A.M. Bennett and his curate], two doctors, three widows, and six old maids; one of the widows being all purity and refinement but with no more taste than the white of an egg'.

In Bournemouth, where the Taylors set up permanent home in 1862, Sir Henry became a founder member of the Society for the Prevention of Cruelty to Animals, of which he became president. Visitors to his house included Benjamin Jowett, Master of Balliol College, Oxford; Alfred, Lord Tennyson, and Aubrey de Vere (cousin of Sir Henry's wife Theodosia, q.v.). It was at one of the Taylors' literary gatherings that Sir Percy and Lady Shelley were first introduced to Robert Louis Stevenson – about whom more will be said shortly. In 1872, Sir Henry retired from the Colonial Service. He died on 27 March 1886. Lady Taylor died on 1 January 1891. Both are buried in St Peter's churchyard.

16

Charles Darwin

In September 1862, English naturalist Charles Robert Darwin (born 12 February 1809) travelled to Bournemouth from his home in Kent. Here, he rented Cliff Cottage, Exeter Road – which stood in 3½ acres of wooded grounds – for one month. This was in order that one of his sons might convalesce after an attack of scarlet fever – which his wife Emma, also subsequently contracted. Three years earlier, in November 1859, his work *The Origin of Species by Means of Natural Selection* had been published. It contained the very first explanation of how different species of plants and animals evolve in different ways.

Darwin was disappointed to find that the environs of Bournemouth lacked the types of flora and fauna in which he was interested. To his friend John Lubbock (later Lord Avebury) he wrote, 'I do nothing here except look at a few flowers, and there are very few

Charles Darwin in 1854.

Cliff Cottage, photographed in 1863 by R. Day. (Reproduced by permission of Bournemouth Libraries)

here, for the country is wonderfully barren'. To the botanist J.D. Hooker, he wrote, 'I can find nothing to look at… even the brooks and ponds produce nothing. The country is like Patagonia [a place with which he was familiar, from his legendary voyage on the HMS *Beagle*, 1831-36]'. Darwin died two decades later, on 19 April 1882, aged seventy-three.

By a curious coincidence, four decades after Darwin's visit to Bournemouth, Alfred Russel Wallace, who had come independently to the same conclusion as Darwin in regard to evolution and natural selection, came to live at Old Orchard, Broadstone, near Poole. Wallace died on 7 November 1913, aged ninety.

Lucy Kemp-Welch

Lucy was born in Bournemouth on 20 June 1869. Her father, Edwin Buckland Kemp-Welch, was a solicitor in the firm of Witt and Kemp-Welch of Market Street, Poole. Her mother was Elizabeth (née Oakes), who, prior to her marriage to Edwin in 1867, was living with her parents in Great Malvern in Worcestershire. After their marriage, the couple set up home at Beaumont Terrace, Poole Hill, Bournemouth, which is where both Lucy and her sister Edith, who arrived the year after her, were born.

The two girls were educated, initially, by a number of private tutors, before progressing to Faringdon House, a private school also on the Poole Road and run by Mrs and Miss Slade. Lucy's father Edwin, was a natural history enthusiast, and he and she made frequent visits to Hampshire's New Forest. The family also spent holidays there, and Lucy recorded the flora and fauna which she discovered – including the famous New Forest ponies – in her sketchbook.

In 1877, Edwin purchased for Lucy a first edition of the newly-published *Black Beauty* by English novelist Anna Sewell. In that year, he was diagnosed with pulmonary tuberculosis (Anna also suffered from tuberculosis which caused her to be confined to her house for a period of six long years, during which time she wrote the book). *Black Beauty* made a lasting impression on Lucy, who was taking riding lessons at the time, and she identified strongly with Anna's compassionate attitude towards horses.

In about 1879 the family moved to a larger house, 'Dinmore' who on Poole Road and just beyond the county boundary in Dorsetshire. Lucy and Edith, who were both determined to become artists, were now sent to Towerfield School as day pupils. By 1883, when she was only fourteen, Lucy began to exhibit her pictures locally.

Lucy became an expert on the anatomy of the horse, both from her study of her father's zoology books, and also from her visits to the Hospital for Sick Horses at nearby Christchurch, run by veterinary surgeon Mr T.B. Goodall. Lucy also visited the studios of Arthur Batt and Arthur H. Davies, animal painters from the New Forest. In that year, she received her first commission. It was from an art dealer, for a study of three horses' heads, to be painted in oils.

Her father Edwin's health continued to deteriorate and he was forced to give up work. On 6 September 1888, when Lucy was aged nineteen, he died. Shortly afterwards, her mother's health also deteriorated. In 1890, the family relocated to Weston-super-Mare in Somerset, to be near to Lucy's Aunt Janet. For Lucy, an aspiring artist, the move proved to be providential.

Lucy Kemp-Welch with 'Black Prince', her model for 'Black Beauty'.

'Gypsy Horse Drovers'. (Reproduced with the kind permission of Russell-Cotes Art Gallery and Museum)

Aunt Janet told the sisters that a distant cousin of theirs was a student at the Herkomer School of Art in Bushey, Hertfordshire, and she suggested that they too might like to apply. The school was owned and run by Hubert von Herkomer, RA, born 1849 at Waal in Bavaria, and formerly Professor of Art at London's Slade School of Fine Art. In 1907, Herkomer received a knighthood. The sisters duly applied, only to be rejected. However, Herkomer suggested that they join a local art school in order to improve their skills. Accordingly, they enrolled at Bournemouth College of Art under director Macdonald Clarke. A year later, in 1891, they reapplied to the Herkomer school and were accepted.

Herkomer stressed the 'necessity for the most personal consideration of each student's idiosyncrasy'.[1] In other words, he encouraged each student to be an individual. With regard to Lucy, he said, 'Miss Kemp-Welch has developed a talent such as is uncommon in man and quite rare in a woman for animal painting'.[2]

In 1895, Herkomer advised Lucy, who had not as yet been promoted beyond his preliminary class, to submit her work 'The Gypsy Horse-Drovers' to the Royal Academy. To her delight, the picture was accepted for hanging, and purchased by Sir Frederick Harris for the sum of £60, even before the exhibition had opened!

When a relative suggested that the annual Pony Drift – the rounding up of ponies with the purpose of checking their health – might be a suitable subject for a painting, Lucy concurred, and spent two summers making preparatory sketches for the picture 'Colt-hunting in the New Forest'. Brimming with life and energy, it was exhibited at the Royal Academy in 1897. The canvas, 10ft by 5ft, was so large that it had to be transported to the Royal Academy in a huge, wooden box by horse and cart! In the same year, the painting was purchased for the nation by the Chantrey Bequest Fund and put on permanent display in the Tate Gallery.

In 1901, with Lord Dundonald, Commander of Cavalry in the Boer War acting as a model, Lucy painted 'In Sight! Lord Dundonald's Dash on Ladysmith'. The painting also featured Winston Churchill, who had served in that conflict as a newspaper correspondent.

In 1905, when Herkomer resigned as president of his school of art and offered it for sale, Lucy decided to buy it. She renamed it, first, 'The Bushey School of Painting', and subsequently, 'The Kemp-Welch School of Drawing and Painting'. However, although she herself was now head of the school, she devoted the majority of her time to painting, rather than to teaching. In the same year, she held her first exhibition at the Fine Arts Society in Bond Street.

Although Lucy purchased a house at Bushey, she often returned to Bournemouth. Here, the sea was close at hand and both 'Foam Horses' and 'Horses Bathing in the Sea' were inspired by a visit to nearby Parkstone. She also visited Poole, the Isle of Purbeck, and her favourite haunt – the New Forest. She did not make a success of her school of painting at Bushey, and in 1911 she sold the property back to Professor Herkomer, who demolished it. Whereupon, she herself relocated to Rudolph Road, Bushey, and re-established her school there. Now smaller in size, it was renamed by her 'The Kemp-Welch School'.

In 1914, Lucy (together with English painters Alfred Munnings and Lionel Edwards) became a founder member of the Society of Animal Painters and served as its first president. Although Lucy painted cats, chickens, dogs, ducks, seagulls, stags, sheep and even polar bears (at the London Zoo), the horse was her principal pre-occupation. She painted horses

FORWARD!

Forward to Victory
ENLIST NOW

First World War recruitment
poster by Lucy Kemp-Welch.

for their own sake – gypsy horses, horses drinking at a stream in the forest, being ridden for pleasure, or at polo matches. The title of a portrait of donkeys and ponies by Lucy, entitled 'Children of the Forest', reveals exactly how she perceived them – as creatures to be loved and cherished. But she was also mindful of the vital part that horses played in a working capacity, in the life of the country – ploughing, hauling timber, or cartfuls of 'mangel-wurzels' (a variety of beet cultivated as cattle food), or wagons laden with hay across snow-clad fields, or even launching a lifeboat. She attended the races, and the title of her picture 'A Little More and How Much It Is', painted at Goodwood Racecourse, reveals how she empathizes with the horses, as each is forced to make the maximum effort in order to be the first to cross the finishing line.

With the advent of the First World War in 1914, Lucy became engaged in the production of military recruitment posters for the British Army. The war provided further opportunities for 'horse paintings', such as 'Forward the Guns' (exhibited RA 1917), where horses were seen hauling artillery pieces across the battlefield. In fact, Lucy had painted the picture at Bulford Army Camp on Salisbury Plain in Wiltshire, the previous autumn! Mindful of the important contribution made to the war effort by British women, she painted 'Women's Work in the Great War', which included images

'She Chose Me for Her Horse' frontispiece for J.M. Dent's 1915 edition of *Black Beauty*.

'It was Ginger' illustration for *Black Beauty*, 1915.

of a nurse, and of women using agricultural tools and industrial machinery normally used by men.

Lucy was commissioned by publisher J.M. Dent to illustrate that publishing house's 1915 edition of *Black Beauty* – the book which she had so enjoyed as a child. To this end, she selected a horse called 'Black Prince', which she had purchased from Robert Baden-Powell – founder of the Boy Scout Movement – as her model. In 1917, she was elected a member of the Royal Institute of Oil Painters.

In 1922 an altogether different kind of commission arrived: from Princess Marie Louise, granddaughter of Queen Victoria, for her to produce two tiny paintings for Queen Mary's dolls' house at Windsor Castle (designed by Sir Edwin Lutyens in 1920 and built by master craftsmen on a scale of 1:12 for Her Majesty). The works, both in pencil and sepia wash, were called 'The Return from the Fields' and 'The Clearing in the Forest'. The Royal Collection also holds two other works by Lucy: 'A Farm Horse pulling a Plough' and 'Leaders of the Gun Team'. In that year, Lucy renamed her school 'The Kemp-Welch School for Drawing and Painting'.

In the summer of 1926, Lucy closed down her art school. Now, with her sister Edith, she travelled with a caravan attached to her Ford motor car with 'Lord' John Sanger's circus, which was one of the largest of its kind. Here, she enjoyed the nomadic life-style, and the opportunity to paint 'Circus pony-rider' and 'The Rosinback' in which a horse is seen performing equestrian tricks, and also elephants and the big top. Her circus paintings were exhibited at London's Arlington Galleries in 1934 and 1938. She became mentor and

Queen Mary's Doll's House.

friend to the artist Edward Seago, whose favourite subjects were landscapes, seascapes and flowers. Her last New Forest paintings date from 1937.

In 1938, Lucy attended the opening of the Kemp-Welch Senior Council School, Rossmore, Poole, named after her grandfather, the educationalist Martin Kemp-Welch, who died in 1888. She also gave permission for her family coat-of-arms to be depicted on the school badge. On 3 November 1941, Lucy's sister, Edith, died.

In 1949, when Lucy was aged eighty, her painting 'Harvest of the Beech Woods' was exhibited at the Royal Academy. She died at Watford on 28 November 1958 at the age of eighty-nine.

Perhaps Lucy's greatest legacy was the way she portrayed, through her paintings, her attitude to horses, which she summed up thus: 'They were,' she said, 'fashioned by nature and not by man – full of faults, variable, beautiful, and lovable beyond words'. A selection of her paintings may be seen in Bournemouth's Russell-Cotes Art Gallery & Museum.

The Reverend John Keble

English Anglican churchman, poet, and hymn writer John Keble, born on 25 April 1792, came to Bournemouth on 11 October 1865, on account of the ill health of his wife Charlotte (née Clarke), to whom he had been married for thirty years. She suffered from chronic asthma.

Keble, Oxford Professor of Poetry from 1831-41, was the initiator of the Oxford Movement which regarded the Church not simply as 'a merely human institution', but rather one which possessed, 'privileges, sacraments, [and] a ministry ordained by Christ'. He had served as Vicar of Hursley and of nearby Otterbourne in Hampshire for over thirty years. Keble was familiar with Bournemouth; its Vicar the Reverend A.M. Bennett having made the following request to him a decade earlier, on 12 September 1855, in response to a request that he himself had had from C.L. Pannel:

> My dear Mr Keble
>
> The Founder of the Sanatorium has expressed a desire, with which I am quite ready to comply, that there should be a special service at our Church on [the] occasion of the opening, that those engaged in the work may ask God's blessing upon it. I venture to request that you would kindly consent to preach on the occasion, and if you do not object, that Mrs Keble and yourself should be my guests at the Parsonage for as long as you find it convenient.
>
> The institution is to be opened for patients on Monday Oct 1, & the day named for the service is Tuesday Oct 2. It is proposed that the children of the National School should have tea in the Corridor. With kind regards to Mrs Keble.
>
> Believe me, yours gratefully and sincerely,
>
> A. Morden Bennett [1]

Keble acceded to Bennett's request. Neither gentleman was aware, of course, that to invite schoolchildren, or anyone else, for that matter, into a sanatorium was to endanger their health.

Even before he came to Bournemouth, Keble had become not only a friend to Bennett, but also a mentor. For example, on 19 June 1862, Bennett wrote to Keble to say that he was debating whether to apply for the post of Chaplain at Morden College, Blackheath (q.v.); this being, 'a valuable appointment... worth £760 per an [annum]: and a house [provided]'. However, said Bennett '...although I feel that I have a good chance of success if I offer myself as a candidate – yet I cannot come to any other decision than to go on working in the place to which I have been called [i.e. Bournemouth].'[2]

Keble's reply, which was written four days later, advised as follows: 'It seems to me that it would be a thousand pities for you at your age [Bennett was now aged only fifty-four] and with your health [which was excellent] …to quit Bournemouth, your flock and your work, for a comparative sinecure. I do not think you would be comfortable in doing it'.[3] Fortunately, for the people of Bournemouth, Bennett took Keble's advice.

At Bournemouth, the Kebles stayed first at South Cliff Villas, and subsequently at 'Brookside', an imposing property in Exeter Lane, overlooking the Bourne and with sea views. During their time there, Keble read to his wife from the works of novelist Charlotte Yonge (a resident of Otterbourne who was his lifelong friend), and busied himself with his own writings and correspondence.

The Reverend John Keble by George Richmond. (Reproduced by kind permission of the Warden and Fellows of Keble College, Oxford)

Keble worshipped regularly at St Peter's Church, travelling there on foot, occupying a favourite position in the recently built south transept and taking Holy Communion on Sundays and Thursdays. He died at 'Brookside' on 29 March 1866, which was Maundy Thursday. Charlotte died six weeks later, on 11 May. They were buried together in the churchyard of All Saints, Hursley.

In May 1866 the *Bournemouth Parish Magazine* proposed that a memorial 'Te Deum' window be placed in the south wall of the transept of St Peter's Church, in Keble's memory. So successful was the appeal that the money provided for both this, and for other windows in the transept. In the lower right-hand corner of the 'Te Deum' window, Keble himself is depicted, along with the 'Doctors of the Church' (those who the church considers to be of particular importance, especially for their contribution to theological or doctrinal matters).

In 1906, the south transept was transformed into a magnificent side chapel dedicated to the memory of Keble.

The Reverend John Keble depicted on the 'Te Deum' window of St Peter's Church.

19

Thomas and Emma Hardy

English novelist, poet, and dramatist Thomas Hardy (born 1840) and his wife, Emma Lavinia (née Gifford), spent four days in Bournemouth from 12 July 1875. He had married Emma, the daughter of a Devonshire solicitor, on 17 September 1874 at the Church of St Peter, Paddington. In that year, *Far From the Madding Crowd* (his fourth published novel) was published. On the fourth day, the couple departed by boat from Bournemouth Pier to Swanage, where they would live for the next ten months, and where Hardy would complete *The Hand of Ethelberta*.

A poem by Hardy, describing that visit to Bournemouth and entitled 'We Sat at the Window', suggests that even at that early stage, all was not well with his marriage.

> We sat at the window looking out,
> And the rain came down like silken strings
> That Swithin's day. Each gutter and spout
> Babbled unchecked in the busy way
>   Of witless things:
> Nothing to read, nothing to see
> Seemed in that room for her and me
>   On Swithin's day.
>
> We were irked by the scene, by our own selves; yes
> For I did not know, nor did she infer
> How much there was to read and guess
> By her in me, and to see and crown
>   By me in her.
> Wasted were two souls in their prime,
> And great was the waste, that July time
>   When the rain came down

Bournemouth would feature again, this time under the fictitious name 'Sandbourne', in three of Hardy's subsequent novels. *In The Hand of Ethelberta* (1876), 'Sandbourne' is where Christopher Julian, a suitor of Ethelberta Chickerel, a butler's daughter, lives and teaches music. Also, it is from here that Ethelberta's brother Sol, and the Honourable Edgar Mountclere attempt to reach 'Knollsea' (Swanage), 'by the steamer that plies between the

Thomas Hardy. (Dorset County Museum)

Emma Lavinia Hardy (née Gifford). (Dorset County Museum)

two places in the summer months'. This is in an (unsuccessful) effort to prevent Ethelberta from marrying Lord Mountclere, whom Sol despises for being 'part of the useless lumber of our nation'. Afterwards, Ethelberta provides her father with a smart villa at 'Sandbourne' for his retirement.

In *Tess of the D'Urbervilles* (1891), Tess Durbeyfield, daughter of an itinerant dealer, is seduced by Alec D'Urberville, son of a wealthy merchant. She subsequently meets Angel Clare, younger son of a parson, whom she marries. When Tess confesses to Angel that she has had an affair with Alec, he refuses to forgive her and departs for Brazil. Alec now pursues Tess, and they take lodgings at 'The Herons' in 'Sandbourne'. Angel returns to England, discovers Tess's whereabouts, and now it is he who asks her for forgiveness. Tess tells him it is too late. Then she changes her mind and murders Alec – a crime for which she pays the ultimate penalty. 'Sandbourne' also features in *The Well Beloved* (1912).

Sir Merton and Lady Russell-Cotes

Merton Russell-Cotes, son of Samuel Cotes, of Tettenhall, Staffordshire, and his wife Elizabeth, was born on 8 May 1835. Whereas he effected further transformations to the face of Bournemouth, his wife Annie gave the town what was arguably, its finest legacy – a museum and art gallery *par excellence*, containing a priceless collection of paintings, assorted antiquities, ethnographical artefacts, and ceramics which they had collected from all over the world.

Russell-Cotes claimed that he was named after Merton College, Oxford with which his family was associated, and also after a relation of the family of Lord Russell, Duke of Bedford. He went to Glasgow, where, in the hope of entering the medical profession, he spent some years as a student. It was there that he met John King Clark, Esq., a wealthy cotton manufacturer of East Woodside, his wife Emmy, and his daughter Annie Nelson (born 15 July 1835), with whom he fell in love. Unfortunately, however, his medical studies came to an end when he developed a 'slight congestion of the right lung'.[1] It was then decided that he should undertake a sea voyage to Buenos Aires where his family had connections, in order that his health might be restored. He sailed from Liverpool on 10 November 1853.

Shortly after his arrival, Russell-Cotes became manager of Buenos Aires' only English school; its master having fallen sick. He returned home via the Indian Ocean island of Mauritius – which in retrospect he described as 'without exception, the most beautiful in the world' – and the Cape of Good Hope. He and Annie were married on 1 February 1860. She would bear him five children: Ella, Clara, Anita, Charlotte and Herbert Victor.

When Russell-Cotes was appointed Resident Secretary and Superintendent of the Scottish Amicable Society, he and his wife moved to Dublin, where they remained for some years. He subsequently returned to Glasgow, where he became manager of the Royal Hanover Hotel. Sadly, ill health overtook him once more, and he suffered frequent attacks of bronchitis which incapacitated him during the winter months. His doctor, therefore, advised him to search for a suitable home in southern England. He took the advice given, and after visiting various resorts, both on the English mainland and on the Isle of Wight, he and his wife finally arrived in Bournemouth. Here, they met Arthur Briant, who offered to sell them the Bath Hotel, which he owned. The outcome was that Russell-Cotes took possession of the hotel on Christmas Day 1876.

Russell-Cotes described how his 'natural love of art' was stimulated by a visit which he had made at the age of sixteen to London's Great Exhibition, an international exhibition of industry and culture. He himself possessed a, so-called, 'loan collection' of 250 pictures,

Merton Russell-Cotes by John Henry Lorimer, 1895. (Reproduced with the kind permission of Russell-Cotes Art Gallery and Museum)

Annie Russell-Cotes by John Henry Lorimer, 1895. (Reproduced with the kind permission of Russell-Cotes Art Gallery and Museum)

which he was in the habit of lending to various 'Corporation Art Galleries throughout the Kingdom', and which he brought with him to Bournemouth, together with paintings by J.M.W. Turner, Camille Corot, Edwin Long, Edwin Landseer and others. These he hung on the walls of the Bath Hotel. Hence, this typically witty remark, directed by Oscar Wilde – who had stayed at the hotel as a guest - to the Russell-Cotes '…you have built and fitted up with the greatest beauty and elegance, a palace, and filled it with gems of art, for the use and benefit of the public at hotel prices'. As for Annie, she was not only a lover of art, but also a Fellow of the Royal Society of Literature.

When the Duke of Argyll – another guest at the hotel – suggested to Russell-Cotes that he 'invest some capital in the improvement of the property', Russell-Cotes approached Christopher Crabbe Creeke, Bournemouth's Town Surveyor. The outcome was that, having closed for a while for substantial extensions and improvements, the Bath Hotel was reopened on 11 August 1880 by Sir Francis Wyatt Truscott, Lord Mayor of London (who had opened Bournemouth's new pier that same day). It was now renamed the 'Royal Bath Hotel', the Prince of Wales – later King Edward VII – having stayed the night there on 23 September 1856.

Phebe (née Pope), mother of Sir (Edwin) Ray Lankester, President of the Bournemouth Natural Science Society from 1911 to 1913, had this to say of the hotel:

> Every sitting-room has its share of beauty, either on the walls in the shape of first-class pictures, or in cabinets of Dresden, Old Worcester, or Sèvres china, and the Japanese collection which was made by Mr and Mrs Russell-Cotes in Japan would delight the lovers of that form of art and decoration. The mention of this word [Japan] reminds me of the great beauty of the

mural decorations of this wonderful hotel. Every wall, every glass door and every available window are covered with charming designs from the skillful brush of Mr Thomas, an artist who is constantly busy here, and whose eye for colour and appreciation of the effects it can produce are really remarkable. [This was a reference to interior decorator John Thomas, q.v.] The corridors, which are long and spacious, are full of paintings.[2]

The hotel was immensely successful, attracting such visitors as Leopold II, King of the Belgians; Eugenie, France's Spanish Empress; Helena, Duchess of Albany, who was the wife of Queen Victoria's youngest son Leopold, and Benjamin Disraeli, formerly Prime Minister of Britain and now Lord Beaconsfield.

Russell-Cotes became active in local politics, and was particularly anxious to enhance Bournemouth's reputation as a health resort. He campaigned for a railway link between Brockenhurst and Bournemouth – the London-Dorchester line having been completed in 1847 – and was successful in that in 1862, this line was linked to Christchurch, and extended onwards to Bournemouth in 1870.

Russell-Cotes also campaigned for the construction of an undercliff drive and pavilion, through the 'Undercliff Drive, Promenade and Pavilion League'. For such a drive to be created, it was necessary for Sir George Meyrick – 4th Baronet – to agree to vest his rights and interests in the Bournemouth cliffs and foreshore in the Bournemouth Corporation. This he did, by signing a 999-year lease on 20 March 1903. As for the Pavilion, the way forward for this had been cleared, in 1892, with the passing of the Bournemouth Improvement Act.

The sections of the Undercliff Drive were completed as follows: 6 November 1907 – Bournemouth Pier to Meyrick Road; 15 June 1911 – A section west of the Pier; 1912 – A section at Alum Chine, and 3 June 1914 – A continuation of the section to the east of the Pier.

The Undercliff Drive proved to be a great amenity for the town, and 'invalids' were now able to drive along the seafront in their carriages.

In 1902, Russell-Cotes declared to the press that, 'a seaside Pavilion is an absolute necessity,' and in that same year, the Council approved a proposal to erect such a building. However, the wheels turned slowly, and it was not until 1909 that the Council authorized the scheme; the pavilion to be built on the Belle Vue site, which it had purchased the previous year.

Russell-Cotes also advocated the building of a hospital and the creation of an orchestra and a public library. In 1883 he was elected to Bournemouth's Board of Commissioners. When, in March 1891, Bournemouth achieved the status of a Municipal Borough, he presented the town's Council with a mace, and a mayoral badge bearing the motto '*Pulchritudo et Salubritas*' ('Beauty and Health'), and inscribed with the name of Bournemouth's very first Mayor, T.J. Hankinson, who was also Chairman of the Bournemouth Commissioners.

Having been granted a Charter (which constituted the town as a Municipal Borough), Bournemouth was now permitted to hold municipal elections and to apply for the right to assume armorial bearings, which the Charter conceded. Accordingly, the College of Arms devised a coat-of-arms, based on the royal arms of Anglo-Saxon King Edward III ('Edward the Confessor'), in whose desmesne the Bournemouth district once was. It was described as follows:

Quarterly or and azure, a cross flory between a lion rampant, holding between the paws a rose in the first and fourth quarters, six martlets, two, two and two in the second, and four salmons naiant and in pale in the third, all counterchanged. Crest: Upon a mount vert a pine tree proper, in front four roses, fessewise, or. Motto: Pulchritudo et Salubritas.

The rose is both a Royal emblem and the emblem of the county of Southampton, in which Bournemouth was then situated. The pine tree, of course, is highly appropriate for the town, as are the salmon and martlets – sand martins. In 1894, and again in 1895, Russell-Cotes became Mayor of Bournemouth, and his wife Annie, Mayoress.

The Russell-Cotes' home, 'East Cliff Hall', which Russell-Cotes gave to his wife as a birthday present, was completed in 1901. Although the architect was John Frederick Fogerty, Russell-Cotes had a considerable influence on its design. Said he, 'I had made up my mind to construct it architecturally to combine the renaissance with Italian and Old Scottish Baronial style'. Their new home would serve not only to house their growing collection, but also as a place to entertain their guests. For example, in the boudoir, which was adjacent to her bedroom, Lady Russell-Cotes received Princess Beatrice, Queen Victoria's youngest child and wife of Prince Henry of Battenberg.

In the main hall, the embossed, canvas wall-coverings (which occur throughout the house) were produced by decorative designer William Scott Morton at his Albert Works in Edinburgh. Its glass dome 'depicts the wonderful extravaganza of a night sky with bats, owls, stars and comets'.[3] The frieze around the top of the stairwell is a replica of the frieze in Greece's Parthenon, which runs around the internal walls of the *cella* (sanctuary

Bournemouth's coat-of-arms. (Bournemouth Borough Council)

containing a statue of the goddess Athena). Around the gallery above, pictures hung from floor to ceiling.

The dining room is the principal room on the ground floor. Here, peacocks and poppies are displayed on a colourful frieze. Four stained-glass windows depict the four saints of the United Kingdom, whilst others depict the crests of arms of Australia, Ceylon, Gibraltar, The Cape, and Malta. Adjacent to it is the conservatory.

The Moorish Alcove connects the study, boudoir, and yellow room – which was Lady Russell-Cotes' bedroom. In it are incorporated designs from the Alhambra Palace and Fortress, built by the Moors in Granada, Spain, which the Russell-Cotes visited in 1910 and described as, 'marvellously beautiful'. At the base of the alcove's domed ceiling is a quotation in Arabic from the Koran, which is repeated twelve times and which translates to, 'There is no conqueror but God'.

The Russell-Coteses were friends of the Shelleys of Boscombe Manor, in whose theatre Henry Irving, the most famous English actor of the day, often performed. Russell-Cotes described Irving's portrayal of Othello in Shakespeare's play *Othello, the Moor of Venice*, thus 'His altercation with Iago was so realistic and terribly intense that it almost made my hair stand on end; in the scene where he smothers Desdemona he has left such a powerful impression on our minds [that] we could not possibly sleep during the night.'[4]

When Irving died in 1905, Russell-Cotes purchased many of his belongings (which were sold at auction) for his museum at East Cliff Hall. They included the skull that the great actor used in his portrayal of Hamlet, in Shakespeare's play of the same name.

East Cliff Hall, aside from the treasures contained therein, was an extravaganza of light and colour, and once again, it was John Thomas who executed the murals and stencils in the majority of its rooms.

The collection which Russell-Cotes and his wife so painstakingly built up during their extensive travels abroad was a reflection of their tastes. Their eye for beauty is reflected in the inscription above the arch in the gallery: 'The eye rejoices in the beautiful from hour to hour'. There are animal paintings, including depictions of dogs, deer, parrots, toucans, cockatoos and macaws. There are sculptures of English soldier and statesman Oliver Cromwell, Admiral Horatio Nelson, engraver John Landseer, and French Emperor Napoleon Bonaparte, and a full-length portrait of Sir Henry Irving in his role as King Charles I by James Archer RSA. There are many sculptures of nudes, which are also depicted in paintings such as 'The Dawn of Love' by English painter William Etty, 'which scandalized many Victorians'.[5] In the main, however, the collection reflected the popular, contemporary taste for art of the Victorian/Edwardian period – Russell-Cotes being especially devoted to the works of English orientalist and romanticist painter Edwin Longsden Long.

Russell-Cotes and his wife Annie's pride in the empire which Britain had created did not prevent them from being curious about other faiths and cultures. Annie, for example, was a founder member of both the Japan and Ethnographical Societies. Their collection of Japanese armour was made during their visit to Japan in 1885. Specimens of kiwi and lyre birds, and a complete Maori war canoe, were acquired on their visit to the Antipodes in 1885.

In 1908, in recognition of their contribution to the life of Bournemouth, the Russell-Cotes' were made Honorary Freemen of the Borough of Bournemouth. For Lady

East Cliff Hall, 1900. (Courtesy of Bournemouth Libraries)

Coving, decorated by John Thomas, in the study of East Cliff Hall. (Reproduced with the kind permission of Russell-Cotes Art Gallery and Museum)

Russell-Cotes' part, she donated, in the same year, East Cliff Hall and its contents to the Mayor and Burgesses of the Borough of Bournemouth. (The proviso being that she and her husband could continue to live there until their deaths). They also provided a fund to support what would now become an art gallery and museum, which was officially opened to the public in 1909 – the year in which King Edward VII bestowed a knighthood on Russell-Cotes. They also financed an extension to the building, which was opened in 1919.

Lady Russell-Cotes died on 17 April 1920, aged eighty-four. The Blue Bedroom subsequently became the 'Mikado's Room', in which were displayed artefacts from the Russell-Cotes' visit to Japan. Russell-Cotes himself died on 27 January 1921, aged eighty-five. Both he and his wife are buried in the mausoleum at Wimborne Road Cemetery.

The Russell-Cotes Art Gallery and Museum opened officially to the public on 10 March 1922. What had been East Cliff Hall's library now became a museum, dedicated to Sir Henry Irving.

Russell-Cotes did not live to see the completion of all of his favourite projects – the Bournemouth Pavilion, for example, for it was not until the winter of 1928/29 that the Belle Vue Hotel was demolished to make way for it. The Pavilion was designed by G. Wyville Home and Shirley Knight. It was opened by the Duke of Gloucester on 19 March 1929.

In 1930-31 the Alum Chine section of the Undercliff Drive ('Promenade') was linked to the Pier section. In 1950, it was extended beyond Boscombe Pier to Sea Road, Southbourne.

During the Second World War, the Royal Bath Hotel was requisitioned for the use of Canadian and RAF officers. In 1963, the hotel owner Phyliss Lee Duncan, Russell-Cotes' granddaughter, sold the hotel to the De Vere group.

When Shaun Garner, Curator of the Russell-Cotes Art Gallery and Museum, was researching the decoration of East Cliff Hall, he recalled seeing an image of a peacock in a Portfolio of Japanese Sketches by John Thomas, dated 1873-75 and published in monochrome by Lethem Brothers of Manchester. (Russell-Cotes possessed no less than three copies of this portfolio by Thomas, which are now in the collection of the Russell-Cotes Art Gallery & Museum). Little is known about Thomas, who in 1898 was employed by the Russell-Cotes to create a 'Japanese Drawing Room' in their Royal Bath Hotel, and also to decorate the walls, covings, and glass of East Cliff Hall. In Thomas's portfolio are depicted such subjects as birds, animals, flowers, courtiers and scenes from Japanese mythology, and Garner realized that it was this which he used as a basis for his hand-painted interior designs.

In 1989, an extension was added to the west side of the Russell-Cotes Art Gallery & Museum, to which writer, photographer, and broadcaster Lucinda Lambton gave the following glowing accolade. Said she, 'there are few, if any, museums worldwide that give me such breadth of cheering delight, surprise, and interest'.

21

Lillie Langtry

Lillie Langtry came to live in Bournemouth, incognito, in 1877 as the mistress of the Prince of Wales. She was born Emilie Charlotte Le Breton (on 13 October 1853) at the rectory of St Saviour's Church, St Saviour, on the Channel Island of Jersey, where her father, the Very Reverend William Corbet Le Breton, held the position of Rector. He was also Dean of Jersey.

The Reverend Le Breton had met, fallen in love with, and married Emilie Davis (née Martin, a widow) during his curacy of St Olave's Church, Southwark, London. Emilie was the second youngest of their seven children; all her siblings being male. Early in life she was nicknamed 'Lillie', 'on account of my skin being unusually white…'.[1]

Lillie had a number of suitors, but, said she, 'Like any other girl I began to dream of the real Prince Charming who would one day appear'. In 1872, when she was aged eighteen, he did appear, in the person of twenty-six-year-old Edward Langtry, an Irishman from Belfast and a widower. However, Lillie's feelings for him appear to be more materialistic than romantic:

> One day there came into the harbour a most beautiful yacht. To become the mistress of the yacht, I married the owner, Edward Langtry.[2]

Langtry, who was in the habit of paying frequent visits to Jersey, invited Lillie and her father to cruise with him on his yacht *Red Gauntlet*. He and Lillie were subsequently married in her father's church, St Saviour's, on 9 March 1874. Two years later, when Lillie was taken seriously ill with an attack of typhoid fever, her physician ordered a change of air. Whereupon, she and her husband – against his wishes – moved to London. This decision, she said, was to have, 'the most momentous effect on my life', 'invitations to receptions and balls were so numerous that we were mostly obliged to attend two or three of each in an evening in order to keep our engagements.'[3]

Lillie's fame as a great beauty quickly spread, and notable artists of the day queued up to paint her. Irish writer, poet, and wit Oscar Wilde, whom she met, said of her, 'I would rather have discovered Lillie Langtry than to have discovered America. She is quite simply the most beautiful woman in the world'.

However, for Lillie, an even more momentous experience was in store. Said she 'It was one evening, late in June [1877], during my first season and at a supper given by Sir Alan Young, the Arctic explorer, that I first met His Majesty King Edward, then Prince of Wales.

In fact, at that supper, Lillie found herself seated next to the Prince. Overcome by the occasion, she was able to converse only in monosyllables. [4] From now on, she and Langtry embarked on a giddy social round of dinner parties, race meetings, visits to operas, concerts, and the theatre, and to yachting regattas, during the course of which she intermingled with the very cream of society. This included, of course, the Prince of Wales and his wife, Princess Alexandra (whom he had married in 1863). Said Lillie, 'this orgy of convivial gatherings… at first seemed to me a dream, a delight, a wild excitement, and I concentrated on the pursuit of amusement with the whole-heartedness that is characteristic of me….'

Lillie now became the Prince's mistress. She rode with him in Hyde Park, and from May 1877, followed his 'unvarying annual routine'. [5] This involved spending the summer in London; August in Cowes, Isle of Wight, for the yachting; October in Scotland for the grouse shooting; winters at Sandringham, and March in France's capital city Paris, and on the French Riviera.

Anxious to spend time with Lillie away from the prying eyes of the public, the Prince of Wales, in 1877, purchased a plot of land in a secluded area near Bournemouth's East Cliff, and told Lillie that here, she could design a home for them both and furnish it as she chose. Lillie called it 'The Red House', owing to the reddish colour of its bricks, and everything about it indicated that it was designed to be a place of welcome for Edward. On the exterior wall were the words '*Dulce Domum*' – 'Sweet Home', and also '*Stet Fortuna Domus*' – 'May Fortune Attend Those Who Dwell Here'.

Inside were similar symbols of love and devotion: a stained-glass window depicting a pair of amorous swans; a corner bath in Lillie's suite, which was in the shape of a heart; a carved, oak fireplace in Edward's suite, which featured hand-painted blue and white tiles, depicting scenes from Shakespeare's plays – a reflection of the couple's love for the theatre. Finally, inscribed in gold lettering on the balcony in the dining room were the words, 'They say – What say they? Let them say' - an indication that the couple cared not a jot what the outside world thought of their liaison. However, the fact that in Bournemouth's Register of Leaseholders, Lillie's name was given as Emilie Charlotte Langton (the surname being a fictitious one), indicates that whilst residing in that town, she was required to remain anonymous.

Other features of The Red House were the unusually high ceiling in the Prince of Wales' suite, deliberately designed so that the concentration of smoke from his cigars might be more readily dissipated. Also on the first floor, above the dining hall, was a peephole through which he could view his guests before deciding whether to descend for his meal! The Prince, however, could not have known that during this time, Lillie was in secret communication with her childhood sweetheart who had remained on the Island of Jersey. More will be said about this shortly.

In 1878, during Lillie's second London season, she was presented to Queen Victoria – her husband Langtry having been presented to Her Majesty two months previously. Lillie remarked that at her presentation there was, 'not even a flicker of a smile upon her [Queen Victoria's] face, and she looked grave and tired', which was hardly surprising, given the circumstances!

Meanwhile, for Lillie, clouds were appearing on the horizon. As her husband Langtry's income from his neglected Irish estates dwindled almost to nothing, so her expenditure on

The Prince of Wales (later King Edward VII) and Lillie Langtry (right). (Langtry Manor)

The King's Chamber at Langtry Manor. (Langtry Manor)

costumes and on her social life was taking its toll of the family's finances. Meanwhile, the Prince of Wales's attention was taken by French actress Sarah Bernhardt, who had arrived in London for the 1879 season. The following year Lillie, for her part, met and fell in love with Prince Louis of Battenberg, born in Austria and a distant cousin of Prince Edward. Her husband Langtry, however, refused to consent to a divorce.

In October 1880, Langtry was declared bankrupt. Lillie was now pregnant, allegedly with Prince Louis' child. She returned to her parents' home in Jersey, from where she travelled to Paris for the confinement. The Prince of Wales, despite the fact that his amorous intentions were now directed elsewhere, supported Lillie both emotionally and financially (albeit indirectly) throughout this period. Meanwhile, the unknowing Langtry was dispatched to America.

When Lillie gave birth to a daughter, Jeanne Marie (born on 8 March 1881), she was attended by a doctor, paid for by the Prince of Wales, who had also paid for her accommodation in the French capital. She now returned to London. Jeanne, however, was sent to The Red House, there to be looked after by Lillie's mother and concealed from Langtry, who was to be kept in ignorance of her existence. Lillie commemorated the birth with a small stained-glass leaded window, which she positioned halfway up the upper staircase at The Red House. As for Jeanne, she was brought up to believe that Langtry was her father and that Lillie was her aunt. Meanwhile, the hapless Langtry spent his time fishing and drinking to excess.

Shunned by London society, Lillie fought her way back into public life by cultivating the friendship of British Prime Minister W.E. Gladstone. It was Oscar Wilde who suggested to her that she could find a way out of her financial problems by becoming an actress. This she did, with the help of an established actress Henrietta Hodson. Meanwhile, Gladstone gave her a piece of advice: 'In your professional career you will receive attacks, personal and critical, just and unjust. Bear them, never reply, and, above all, never rush into print to explain or defend yourself'.[6]

Lillie's first successful role came in December 1881, when she played Kate Hardcastle in Oliver Goldsmith's play *She Stoops to Conquer*. For its matinée performance at the Haymarket Theatre, the Prince and Princess of Wales were present in the Royal Box. Another source of income for Lillie was in the world of advertising. For example, she agreed to her name and likeness being used for a full-page advertisement for Pears' Soap. This appeared in the *Illustrated London News*, for which she was paid the sum of £132.

In 1882, having let The Red House, Lillie sent Jeanne to Jersey, to be looked after in a rented cottage by her mother and a maid, Dominique. That October, she, and a theatre company which she had created, toured the USA with a repertoire of plays, including ones by Shakespeare, Goldsmith, Shaw and W.S. Gilbert.

In 1883, Lillie, with a diamond ring – which had undoubtedly been given to her by the Prince of Wales – lovingly scratched the letters 'E' and 'ELL' onto the pane of a downstairs window at The Red House, together with a pair of intertwined hearts, a cupid's arrow, and the date. The 'E' stood for Edward, and the 'ELL' for Emilie (Lillie's first name) Le Breton (her maiden name) and Langtry (her married name).

In 1885, Lillie and her company opened the season at London's new Prince Edward Theatre (named in honour of the Prince of Wales). In 1886, and again in 1887, she embarked on further tours of the USA. In the latter year, she obtained a divorce from Langtry.

In 1888, on the death of Lillie's father, William Le Breton, Lillie's mother and daughter moved in with her at 2 Cadogan Place, London – a property bought for her by the Prince of Wales, with whom a cordial relationship continued to exist. (Lillie subsequently built a Tudor-style home for her widowed mother in the grounds of The Red House. This she subsequently sold to a clergyman, who inhabited it for the next thirty years or so, after which it became a hotel).

Lillie as Shakespeare's 'Cleopatra'. (Langtry Manor)

In 1889, Lillie took a two-year lease of London's St James's Theatre, and over the next decade her career continued to flourish. Also, she became a successful racehorse owner and breeder: her horse 'Merman' winning the Cesarewitch on 12 October 1897, and a prize of £120,000, after which the Prince of Wales paid her the compliment of escorting her into the Jockey Club Enclosure. Two days later, her husband Langtry died in Chester Asylum for the Insane (to which he had been admitted ten days previously). Lillie sent a wreath of flowers, but did not attend the funeral.

Langtry's death gave Lillie the opportunity to take Jeanne into her confidence, and reveal to her that she was her mother, and not her aunt. However, Jeanne continued to believe that Langtry was her father.

On 27 July 1899, Lillie married Hugo Gerald de Bathe, who would inherit a baronetcy. The marriage took place at St Saviour's Church, Jersey, where her father had been Rector and where she had married Langtry. He was aged twenty-seven and she forty-seven. When the Boer War began, Hugo joined the British Army in South Africa and Lillie returned to the London stage.

In January 1901, Queen Victoria died at the age of eighty-one and Edward finally acceded to the throne as King Edward VII. By now, Lillie's fortunes had changed so much that she was able to purchase the lease of the Imperial Theatre and spend almost £50,000 on its refurbishment. In June 1902, on the night before her marriage to Scotsman Ian Malcolm, Lillie's daughter, Jeanne, learned that Prince Louis, and not Langtry, was her father. Having now been doubly deceived as to her parentage, Jeanne broke with her mother, telling Lillie, 'In future, we had best live our own lives apart'. Lillie was distraught.[7]

In the spring of 1905, Lillie embarked on a theatrical tour of South Africa. In late October 1906, she made her first appearance in vaudeville at the 5th Avenue Hotel, New York. In 1907, her husband Hugo's father died, whereupon Hugo became Sir Hugo, and Lillie, Lady de Bathe.

King Edward VII died on 6 May 1910, following an attack of bronchitis. Lillie did not attend the funeral, but observed the procession from the balcony of the Berkeley Hotel. In memory of Lillie's friendship with Edward, his widow Queen Alexandra, gave her custody of his wire-haired fox terrier 'Caesar'.

In 1913, Lillie tried her hand at being a film actress, but this venture was not a success. During the First World War she fulfilled engagements in the USA, where she, 'took part in benefits for the wounded [service personnel] in most of the big cities…'.[8] She did the same in the United Kingdom, and also donated the profits from her production of her play *Mrs Thompson* by Sidney Grundy (which was produced both in London and in New York) to the Red Cross.

In 1918, Lillie retired from the stage. Her last place of residence, the Villa Le Lys ('House of the Lily'), was situated above the cliffs at Monaco. Here, she made a beautiful garden (which in 1924, won the prize for the best on the Riviera). Her husband, Hugo, also lived in Monaco, but by now, the couple had become estranged.

In 1928, Lillie met her youngest grandchild, Mary Malcolm, for the first time. Later, her two eldest grandsons were permitted, by their mother Jeanne, to visit her and to stay with her at Villa Le Lys. Lillie died there, on 12 February 1929, at the age of seventy-five. Her body was brought back to Jersey and interred in St Saviour's churchyard.

Lillie had lived her life as an opportunist, and if fame, fortune or excitement beckoned, then this is the direction that she took, irrespective of the conventions of the day. For example, she had a string of affairs, declined to wear corsets and camisoles, and was one of the first women to smoke cigarettes in public, and to exhibit painted fingernails! But was she ever truly happy? Who knows? Certainly, she fulfilled her early dream of finding 'excitement' and 'amusement'. Looking back on her life, she said, 'I have all that I really wanted very much – a yacht, a racing stable, a theatre of my own, a lovely garden'.[9] But was this the whole truth? Did she not crave happiness on a deeper, more emotional level?

In 1978, sixty-five letters written by Lillie were discovered by Jersey resident Anthony Le Gallais, in the attic of a house on the island which belonged to his aunt. They were contained in a small green box, and had been written between 1878 and 1882, when Lillie was living in Bournemouth. The recipient was Arthur Clarence Jones, born 12 March 1854.

Arthur was the illegitimate child (one of the seven) of Lord Ranelagh of Ranelagh House, Fulham, and Mary Edwards Elliot of Westminster.[10] Ranelagh had an estate at Portelet, Jersey, which is where Arthur and his siblings used to spend the summer months, often in the company of Lillie and her siblings (Ranelagh being a friend of Lillie's father William).

Lillie's letters to Arthur leave the reader in no doubt that she and he were lovers. For example, they contain such phrases from Lillie as:

Darling, come up for a minute when you come [presumably to London]. Ned [Langtry's nickname] has actually gone out for half an hour so if you come soon I shall see you alone. Do you like the letter case? [Presumably, this was the small green box referred to above]. I hope it isn't too large. Your lover ever, Lillie. [and again] If I can also escape Ned I also will come down by the 12.10 [train].[11]

When Lillie discovers that she is pregnant (with Jeanne), it is to Arthur that she first turns: 'What am I to do darling? I am so worried… If you love me you can't be so unkind as to leave me. You dear, you know I care for you only in the world, but I hardly dare look at you'. And later, 'Dearest boy I hope you miss me. Please please hurry back I want you so much'.[12]

In the autumn of 1882, Lillie told Arthur, who the previous year had travelled to Paris to be with her during her confinement, that she missed him 'dreadfully much….' She wrote

Arthur Clarence Jones. (Anthony Le Gallais)

The box, discovered by Anthony Le Gallais, which contained Lillie's love letters from Arthur Jones. (Anthony Le Gallais)

to him again, 'How I wish my darling you could make some money; enough for us to be happy. I am so miserable tonight, I feel I can't live without you.'[13] Arthur, although he was of independent means, was evidently not in a position to support her, or at any rate, not in the style to which she was accustomed!

Twelve years later, on 28 March 1894, Arthur married Maria (née Daniel), widow of Herbert Crawshay, in Biarritz, where the former had become Master of Hounds. In this capacity, he in all probability met King Edward VII, who was a frequent visitor to the French resort, and also a keen huntsman. In 1901, Arthur and Maria's son, Arthur Heron Jones, was born.

Notwithstanding the fact that Lillie's former sweetheart was now a married man, Lillie often went to stay with Arthur and Maria, in a room set aside for her in the house where they lived at Portelet. Arthur died in about 1920, and Maria in 1942.[14]

In 1977, the Manor Heath Hotel, as The Red House had now become, was acquired by Mrs Pamela Howard, who changed its name to the 'Langtry Manor', and, to her great credit, restored it to its former glory. Notably, she uncovered its original wallpaper, and also the stunning fireplace in Edward's bedroom. As for the house which Lillie had built for her mother in the grounds, this has since been converted into flats, known as 'Langtry House'.

The hotel, which is now run by Pamela's daughter, Tara, won this accolade from *Out and About* magazine: 'Very occasionally you stumble upon a rare gem of a hotel where the building, food, service, and history blend to form something quite exceptional. Such is the Langtry Manor Hotel in Bournemouth.'

Dr Horace Dobell and his wife Elizabeth

Horace Benge Dobell, born 1 January 1828, and his wife Elizabeth, came to Bournemouth to take up permanent residence at 'Streate Place', St Peter's Road, in October 1882. Prior to that, he had been Physician, and subsequently Consulting Physician, to the Royal Hospital for Diseases of the Chest, London, during which time, he, and other physicians, had sent many of their patients to Bournemouth for the benefit of their health.

On his arrival in Bournemouth, Dobell declared, 'I did not come here, as many have done, for the purpose of making a fortune, or even to earn a living…'. His aim, he said, 'aside from getting out of the "hurly burly" of London,' was to seek, 'some calm and learned leisure after an arduous career'. Now, his only wish was '…to perform the simple and pleasant task of laying before my professional brethren, without prejudice on one side or the other, an independent and carefully considered account of the medical aspects of Bournemouth and its surroundings'.

This he did in his book, *The Medical Aspects of Bournemouth and its Surroundings*, published in 1886, which he dedicated to Dr W.S. Falls, Junior Physician from 1862, and to Dr W. Allis Smith, Surgeon from 1862 of the National Sanatorium.

Dobell paid tribute to Bournemouth's early planners for building houses on top of the cliffs, where the air was 'less moist and less strongly saline' than at their base. In addition, it was his opinion that chines had, 'a very potent influence for good, in addition to the beauty which they give to the scenery', for they served to drain the water off the cliffs and into the sea, and formed channels, 'by which the sea breezes are allowed to penetrate among the houses inland'. This was especially true of the largest chine – known as 'The Valley of the Bourne' (Bourne Chine). In possessing an abundance of pine trees, 'Bournemouth has a further great advantage over all other English watering places'. This was because of the:

> …resinous perfume, and balmy, incense-like odour which pervades the air [which was] considered to be so beneficial to consumptives [tuberculous patients] and persons suffering from bronchial infections…
>
> Also, the trees in and around the town afforded, 'the most complete shelter from the cold blasts of winter, and delightful shade and coolness in summer…'[1]

Dobell's wife was Elizabeth Mary (née Fordham) of Odsay House, Cambridgeshire, born on 8 March 1828. Brought up in a Hertfordshire manor house, she was the sixth child in a family of five sons and four daughters. Her house possessed an excellent library, and she had been interested in books and poetry from an early age. In fact, she went on to become a poet herself.

When Elizabeth's eldest brother was dying from consumption, she nursed him for many months until the end. She did the same for her youngest brother, who suffered the same fate, 'after lingering for some years at home'.[2] Elizabeth herself suffered several protracted attacks of haemoptysis (the coughing up of blood from the lungs), which is symptomatic of tuberculosis, and she was considered fortunate not to have been laid low by the disease herself.

A happy event, however, occurred when Elizabeth's sister Emily married the poet Sydney Thompson Dobell, for it was at the couple's wedding that she met Sydney's brother Horace. It was, said Elizabeth, 'a remarkable instance of true love at first sight'. Horace was a medical student and Elizabeth described how, in one of his vacations, she took a pony ride with him through the Gloucestershire countryside. Having stopped at a church, of which they decided to make a sketch, they happened to notice a tablet on the church wall which recorded the deaths of seven brothers and sisters, from the same family, all of whom died from consumption. This led Elizabeth to remember what her own family had suffered in this regard, and to give, 'vent to her feelings of the uselessness of doctors and the emptiness of their professed powers'. Whereupon, Horace asked, 'What if he should devote his life to discovering a cure for this scourge?' She wholeheartedly concurred, and this was the goal which he now set for himself.[3]

Elizabeth and Dobell were married on 5 July 1849. On 7 September 1850, she gave birth to a daughter Mary, who was followed by Violet and Horatia. A decade later, in 1859, having qualified as a doctor, Dobell became Physician to London's Royal Hospital for Diseases of the Chest, which '…led to his introducing to the medical profession, in 1863, the use of pre-pancreatised foods in the treatment of consumption and other wasting diseases; by which a complete revolution was effected in the feeding of the sick'.[4]

It was on the occasion of a 'flying visit' to Bournemouth by the Dobell's in September 1880, that Elizabeth wrote her poem *By the White Cliffs.*

> White cliffs that breast the ocean wave,
> Fringed with dark shades of birch and pine,
> Bright stars that light the pirate's cave,
> And through their gloomy branches shine;
> Flag of the yacht, or idler's sail
> That gently flaps the dying gale,
> Across the darkness ye return,
> Like visions – mournful, but not stern.

Dobell encouraged his wife – who suffered recurrent bouts of ill health – to make a collection of her poems for publication. They were duly published by Keegan Paul in early 1881. By this time, her second child ,Violet, had married Dr Charles M. Tidy, a Harley Street physician by whom she had two children. When Violet developed a 'chronic internal disease', the Dobells decided to take her to their house in Bournemouth, in the

'He Giveth His Beloved Sleep' – Elizabeth Mary
Dobell in 1851, aged twenty-three, from a pencil
sketch by her husband.

Elizabeth Dobell, aged thirty-seven, from a
portrait by J. Archer.

hope that the change would do her good. Sadly, this was not to be the case, and Violet
died on 29 July 1881. In the sacrarium of St Peter's Church, Bournemouth, the Dobells
placed a monument tablet, 'beneath a fresco emblematic of the Christian virtues', in their
daughter's memory. Following this tragic event, said Dobell, he and his wife decided to
spend the remainder of their lives in Bournemouth, 'amidst new thoughts, new scenes, and
new spheres of work'.

Dobell described the 'emanations from the pines', such as were to be found at
Bournemouth, as being both 'antiseptic and balsamic',[5] and he was suspicious of those
who discredited 'the idea of the importance of the pine woods and plantations' to health,
believing that such people were speculators, anxious to get rid of the trees in order to
build houses on the site. He was also wise enough to realize that diseases of the lung could
not be cured by climate alone, but nonetheless, climate could be, 'a more or less powerful
adjuvant to other medical treatment...'[6]

It was in Bournemouth, he said, that he, 'originated the design of bringing to this
country the system of treatment known in the Auvergne as the "Mont Dore Cure"'. And
of the diseases which Dobell had in mind to treat, pulmonary tuberculosis was probably
the most prevalent.

It was English physician Dr Richard Morton, who, in 1689, associated the pulmonary
form of the disease which became known as tuberculosis with the existence of 'tubercles',
rounded nodular lesions, in the lungs. However, it was not named tuberculosis until 1839,
by German professor, Johann Lukas Schönlein. On 24 March 1882, the year in which
Dobell and his wife came to live in Bournemouth, German physician Robert Koch

identified mycobacterium tuberculosis as the bacillus which caused tuberculosis, for which he received the Nobel Prize.

In 75 per cent of tubercular patients, the infection is confined to the lungs, causing chest pain, a productive and prolonged cough lasting more than three weeks, and haemoptosis (the coughing up of blood). This is accompanied by fever, night sweats, loss of appetite, weight loss, pallor and fatigue. In the remaining 25 per cent of patients, the infection spreads from the lungs to other organs.

Writing in November 1884, Dobell looked forward to the opening in Bournemouth of 'two institutions of immense importance'. The first of these was the Bournemouth Sanitary Hospital, which was currently being built (in Gloucester Road, and which opened on 13 January 1886) for the, 'isolation of contagious and infectious diseases...'. The second was the Hotel Mont Dore (named after a similar establishment situated in the Auvergne province of France) 'for the treatment of the rheumatic, gouty, scrofulous, syphilitic, tuberculous, dartrous (a condition which predisposes to certain skin diseases), and other morbid constitutional states; also for asthma, consumption, bronchitis, emphysema, naso-pulmonary catarrh and other infections of the throat, chest and mucous membranes'.[8] In that year, 1884, Scottish writer Robert Louis Stevenson – about whom more will be said shortly - visited Bournemouth and was treated by Dr Dobell.

The foundation stone of the Hotel Mont Dore was laid on 25 May 1881 by HM Oscar II, King of Sweden and Norway. A magnificent building, designed by London architect Alfred Bedborough, it opened its doors on 23 May 1885. Shortly afterwards, an advertisement for the hotel appeared in *The Times* newspaper:

> The Mont Dore' of Bournemouth.
> Residential and Bath Establishment.
> 120 bed and sitting rooms.
> Besides the General Dining, Drawing, Reading, Billiard, and Smoking Rooms, a Fine Music Room, Lawn Tennis Courts &c.

Here was offered not only the so-called 'Mont Dore Cure', but also other state-of-the-art treatments for the wide variety of conditions mentioned above. Salt, Turkish and other baths were situated in the basement, where patients, both resident and non-resident, could luxuriate in either pure fresh water from the adjacent Bourne, or salt water pumped from the sea. For afflictions of the eyes, ears and nose, all the various forms of douche (cleansing by irrigation) were available; also, baths, both 'ordinary' and 'medicated', together with 'extensive halls... set apart for the inhalation of vapourised water'.

Dobell, who can be credited with introducing the 'Mont Dore Cure' to Britain, was anxious that the method of treatment be taught and carried out in the correct manner. It was therefore, at his suggestion, that Dr Alfred Meadows, JP, chairman of the public company created to implement Dobell's grand scheme, visited the Auvergne in person. Here, he made arrangements with Dr Emond, the chief physician to the Mont Dore establishment there, to come and spend the winter season at the Hotel Mont Dore, Bournemouth, where he would carry out the Mont Dore treatment, 'in exact accordance with the method so successfully adopted in France'.[9]

In his book, *Bournemouth as a Health Resort*, A. Kinsey-Morgan, Member of the Sanitary Institute of Great Britain and Bournemouth's Medical Officer of Health, describes the benefits of the 'Mont Dore' treatment, and how good results could be expected for any disease of the naso-pulmonary tract and also for some rheumatic affections.[10]

Whereas in the Auvergne, said Kinsey-Morgan, treatment was only available for three months of the summer, at Bournemouth, the 'Mont Dore Cure' could be administered all year round. 'This is an incalculable advantage, for the treatment is available at the very time at which the patient is most suffering'. He also agreed with M. Boudant, Professor at the School of Medicine, Clermont-Ferrand, who observed that waters exported from the French spa towns of Mont Dore or La Bourboule, could be drunk just as advantageously in Bournemouth and other places, as they could, 'when taken at the source'. Kinsey-Morgan also declared that, 'Stern's Pine Extract made an excellent, refreshing bath and may be used in sea water equally well as in ordinary water at our own homes'.[11] This was a reference to 'Pumiline, the Pure Essence and Extract of Pumilio pine', which was manufactured and sold by G&G Stern of 11 Billiter Square, London, from a variety of pine which grew '…on the higher altitudes of the Alps in regions of perpetual snow [and] constituted the effectual remedy for Gout, Rheumatism, and Throat and Chest Affections'.

Having been used successfully at various health resorts on the Continent, pumiline was first used in Britain at the Hydro-Therapeutic Establishment at Farnborough, Hampshire. According to Walter J. Sykes, MD, not only was 'Pumilio' a '…potent antiseptic, very effectually arresting decomposition… [but] when vapourised it acts as a potent disinfectant and deodorizer, quickly destroying miasmata and other offensive emanations'.[12]

Other physicians who played a part in the treatments offered at Hotel Mont Dore included Dr Isaac Lennox Browne, throat specialist and author of *The Throat and Its Diseases* who, 'constructed a dry inhaler of a novel character' to facilitate the inhalation of Stern's pumiline essence or eucalyptor (extract from the crushed leaves of the eucalyptus tree).[13] Finally massage, carried out by trained masseurs, was offered; its object being '… to raise the tone of the nervous and circulatory systems; to remove morbid congestions… [and relieve] certain forms of gout, rheumatism, and kindred disorders; to allay pain in its various forms.'[14]

Beyond the confines of the Hotel Mont Dore, Dobell had nothing but praise for the local chemists who supplied the 'medicinal foods and appliances' which constituted 'so important a part of treatment', and also for the, 'good medical care' provided by the local medical practitioners.[15] As far as Bournemouth itself was concerned, however, he issued this caveat. Said he:

> In the western part of the town, regular streets and terraces of lodging-houses begin to rise, which seem far more appropriate for Brighton than for Bournemouth. If this suicidal course is persisted in, and the inhabitants aim at building palaces and streets, and cut down their invaluable pine trees without hesitation, Bournemouth will lose all its present beauty and advantages…16

And what of Dobell's wife, Elizabeth? Despite the tragic loss of her daughter, Violet, she appears to be benefiting from her new life by the sea, when, writing in the third person, she declares that:

No event in the life of a poetess [i.e. herself] had so great an influence on her works as this removal to Bournemouth. Always an ardent lover of the countryside… yet for thirty-two years, taking her place in 'London society'… she now returned to the country with delight. Note that at that time, Elizabeth regarded Bournemouth as being part of the countryside! Likewise, her poem 'In the Watches of the Night', reflects her thoughts about her chosen new abode:

Oh! In the calm, the wonderful sweet calm
Of these old woods, that seem so strangely far
From turmoil and from grief – that have a balm
To heal the wounded soul – and where the star
Of evening looks into uplifted eyes,
And where the deep roar of Earth's cities dies…

She waxes lyrical about her new home, 'Streate Place', with its beautiful trees and garden, set within the sound of the sea, 'and of those lovely "Italian moonlights"' for which Bournemouth 'is distinguished', and declares 'this was exactly what both heart and mind had craved for, after all that had passed in the last twelve years of sickness, anxiety, and grief. It had a marvellous effect on restoring both physical and nervous health'.

In 1892, the Dobells relocated to Parkstone Heights, Constitution Hill in neighbouring Poole. Elizabeth died on 1 August 1908, and her husband on 22 February 1917. They are buried in Parkstone Cemetery.

The Hotel Mont Dore. (Reproduced by permission of Bournemouth Libraries)

276　THE CHEMISTS' AND DRUGGISTS' DIARY, 1894

PUMILINE.

Essence 1/6 ...	Per dozen, 15/-, less 10 per cent.	Liniment 1/9 ...	Per dozen, 20/-, less 10 per cent.
„ 2/6 ...	„ 24/- „ 10 „	Jujubes 1/1 ...	„ 10/6 „ 5 „
Extract 1/- ...	„ 9/- „ 10 „	„ 2/3 ...	„ 20/- „ 5 „
Ointment 1/1½ ...	„ 11/- „ 10 „		
„ 2/9 ...	„ 27/- „ 10 „	Dry Inhalers, complete 1/6 „	14/- „ 10 „

G. & G. STERN, 62 GRAY'S INN ROAD, LONDON, W.C.

'Pumiline' advert.

During the First World War, the Hotel Mont Dore was requisitioned by the government as a hospital for Indian forces, and later for British service personnel. It subsequently became a convalescent home for British officers. In 1920, it was purchased by the Council for the sum of £33,000, to serve as Bournemouth's third Town Hall, which opened officially on 1 October 1921. In 1931, work was begun on a new Council Chamber, which opened the following year. A two-storey office block with car park was opened in 1972. In 1992, another extension, costing £6 million, was opened.

23

Robert Louis and Fanny Stevenson

Writer and poet Robert Louis Balfour Stevenson, born on 13 November 1850 at 8 Howard Place, Edinburgh, came to Bournemouth with his wife Fanny in July 1884, and remained here until August 1887. It was here that he was to write some of his most famous works. Aged thirty-three, Stevenson was already a famous author, his book *Treasure Island* having been published in 1883. His father, Thomas Stevenson, was joint engineer to the Northern Board of Lighthouses; his mother was Margaret Isabella Balfour.

Stevenson attended Edinburgh Academy, from which he was frequently absent on account of a chest condition. His first publication, a pamphlet entitled 'The Pentland Rising of 1666' (an account of an uprising in south-west Scotland by 'Covenanters' who wished to preserve Presbyterianism) was printed privately in 1866.

It was hoped that Stevenson would follow the family profession of civil engineering – as a child, he often accompanied his father on official visits to lighthouses on the Scottish coast – and to this end he enrolled, at the age of seventeen, at Edinburgh University to study that subject. His tutor was Fleeming Jenkin, an expert in electrical engineering and a man whom he greatly admired. However, he decided to abandon engineering and take a degree in law instead.

Stevenson made several visits to the Continent, and in particular to the Forest of Fontainebleau near Paris, where he met notable writers and artists of the day. He spent the winter of 1873–74 at Mentone in the French Maritime Alps. In 1875, he was called to the Scottish Bar. However, he never practised as a barrister. By now, he was contributing essays to various periodicals including the *Cornhill Magazine*.

It was in July 1876, at Grez – a village to the south-east of Paris – that Stevenson met his future wife Fanny Vandegrift Osbourne, an American from Oakland, California. He was twenty-five. She was a thirty-six-year-old, separated from her husband and with two children.

Stevenson recorded his adventures in France, Belgium, Germany, and his native Scotland, in such works as *Inland Voyage* (1878) and *Travels with a Donkey in the Cevennes* (1879). On 19 May 1880, in San Francisco he and Fanny were married – she having obtained a divorce. That autumn he returned to Scotland with his wife and stepson, Lloyd Osborne, to live with his parents. He spent the winter 1880 and 1881 at the resort and health spa of Davos in the Swiss Alps, hoping that his health would improve – which it did. However, when he returned to Scotland it deteriorated once more. He therefore, decided to relocate to the south of France. In January 1884, he suffered a serious relapse from which he almost died.

Robert Louis Stevenson.

Stevenson, like many others, chose Bournemouth as a place to live because of its congenial atmosphere, and the fact that here were to be found experts in the treatment of chest diseases, and consumption in particular (from which Stevenson was known to be suffering). Another factor was that his stepson Lloyd Osborne, was currently attending school in the town. Having arrived in Bournemouth in the summer of 1884, the Stevensons resided briefly at 'Iffley', a boarding house in West Cliff Road, before moving to 'Wensleydale' in the same road, where they stayed for six weeks or so. In late October or early November 1884, they relocated to 'Bonallie Towers' in Burton Road, Branksome Park.

In the summer of 1885, Stevenson, together with his wife, his stepson, and his cousin Robert A.M. Stevenson visited novelist, poet, and dramatist Thomas Hardy at Max Gate in Dorchester. Stevenson had first met Hardy at the Bloomsbury house of Sir Sidney Colvin, Keeper of Prints and Drawings at the British Museum. Hardy had only recently moved into Max Gate – a house which he had designed himself – and Stevenson was one of his first visitors. As for Stevenson, he was en route to Dartmoor, being desperate to find somewhere where the air would be even more conducive to his health than that of Bournemouth. However, he never reached his destination. Instead, he fell ill at Exeter and remained there until he was well enough to return home.

In Bournemouth, Stevenson began work on *Kidnapped*, a novel describing the adventures of David Balfour following the Jacobite Rebellion of 1745. In 1885, the year after his arrival in the town, *A Child's Garden of Verses* was published. In the same year, following a dream which gave him the idea for the story, Stevenson interrupted his work to write *The Strange Case of Dr Jekyll and Mr Hyde*. Jekyll, a physician, discovers a drug which enables him to create for himself Mr Hyde, a separate persona in which are embodied all Jekyll's evil instincts. Both this novel and *Kidnapped* were published in 1886. In Bournemouth, Stevenson also wrote *Prince Otto* (a romance), *More Arabian Nights*, and, in collaboration with W.D. Henley, three plays: *Beau Austin*, *Admiral Guinea*, and *Robert Macaire*.

In letters, written between July 1884 and August 1887 when he was resident in Bournemouth, Stevenson communicated not only with his parents, but also with a number of literary figures and literary critics including W.E. Henley, the Reverend Professor Lewis Campbell, Charles Baxter, Edmund Gosse, Henry James, Sidney Colvin, J.A. Symonds, W.H. Low, P.G. Hamerton and William Archer. These letters reveal much about Stevenson the man: what his thoughts were, and how he occupied himself at this time. They also reveal emotions that go up and down like a roller coaster, as he delights in his writing and in the success of it on the one hand, whilst on the other, the terrible disease from which he is suffering, continually threatens, and sometimes succeeds, in dragging him down.

On 28 September 1884, Stevenson writes to his parents from 'Wensleydale', Bournemouth, to complain how impoverished he is. 'I find the lockers entirely empty; not a cent to the front. Will you pray send that sum [of money which, presumably, they had offered him]?' And then, commenting on the weather and the local scenery, 'It blows an equinoctial gale, and has blown for nearly a week. Nimbus Britannicus, piping wind, lashing rain; the sea is a fine colour, and wind-bound ships lie at anchor under the Old Harry Rocks, to make one glad to be ashore'.

On 3 October 1884, he writes to his publisher Andrew Chatto (of Chatto & Windus), telling him, 'Your fair, open, and handsome dealings are a good point in my life, and do more for my crazy health than has yet been done by any doctor'.

In November 1884 he demonstrates, in a letter to his father, how not only he, but also Fanny, are suffering on account of his ill health:

Fanny is very much out of sorts, principally through perpetual misery with me. I feel I have been a little in the dumps which, AS YOU KNOW, SIR, is a very great sin. I must try to be more cheerful; but my cough is so severe that I have sometimes most exhausting nights and very peevish wakenings.

To Charles Baxter on 11 November 1884, he writes, 'I put in the dark watches, imitating a donkey [braying – i.e. coughing] with some success, but little pleasure; and in the afternoon I indulge in a smart fever, accompanied by aches and shivers'.

To a Miss Ferrier on 12 November 1884, he reveals just how dreadfully 'consumption' can affect a person, 'I am about knocked out of time now: a miserable, snuffling, shivering, fever-stricken, nightmare-ridden, knee-jottering, host-hosting shadow and remains of a man'. Nevertheless, he is determined not to give way to his illness, telling her – in his own, Scottish vernacular – 'We'll no gie ower jist yet a dittie'. ('We will not give over just yet a while'.)

On 9 December 1884, he tells his parents that he is still in dire financial straits, 'About money, I am afloat and no more, and I warn you, unless I have great luck, I shall have to fall upon you at the New Year like a hundredweight of bricks. Doctor, rent, chemist, are all threatening; sickness has bitterly delayed my work; and unless, as I say, I have the mischief's luck, I shall completely break down'.

And then, pathetically, 'If only I had a halfpenny worth of health, I could now easily suffice'. And yet his enthusiasm for his writing never wanes. On 4 January 1885, he tells Sir Sidney Colvin that he is preparing to produce a work about the Iron Duke (Duke of Wellington) for publisher Longman, Green & Company's series English Worthies, for which he will shortly receive a payment of royalties. In February, he tells J.A. Symonds:

My 'Child's Verses' [A Child's Garden of Verses] come out next week. OTTO [a reference to *Prince Otto: A Romance*] begins to appear in April; more ARABIAN KNIGHTS [*More New Arabian Nights*] as soon as possible. Moreover, I am neck-deep in [the Duke of] Wellington; also a story on the stocks, GREAT NORTH ROAD [*A Tragedy of the Great North Road*].

By 12 March, however, his mood has changed, and to his friend, the English poet and critic Edmund Gosse, he shows his frustration at being confined to the house, by signing himself, in capital letters, 'THE HERMIT OF SKERRYVORE'. (Here, he is anticipating a change of address, for four days later, he tells P.G. Hamerton, 'My father has presented me with a beautiful house here – or so I believe, for I have not yet seen it, being a cage-bird, but for nocturnal sorties in the garden'.)

The house to which Stevenson referred, situated at the head of Alum Chine, was originally called 'Sea View' – for obvious reasons. However, Stevenson renamed it 'Skerryvore' – after a lighthouse off the coast of Argyll, Scotland, which his family's firm had designed. At Skerryvore, Stevenson's suffering continued. Coughing up blood, and feeling weak and exhausted, he was virtually confined to the property. Nevertheless, as a lover of classical music, he taught himself to play the piano. Visitors to Skerryvore included Sir Sidney Colvin, the authors Henry James (who stayed for ten weeks) and Thomas Hardy, and Sir Henry and Lady Taylor. Occasionally, Stevenson managed a visit to Boscombe Manor, where Sir Percy and Lady Jane Shelley lived. Here, Sir Percy took his photograph, and Lady Shelley, 'discovering in him a close likeness to her renowned father-in-law [the poet], she forthwith claimed him as her son'.[1]

In June 1885, Stevenson writes to Mrs Fleeming Jenkin, to commiserate with her on the death of her husband, his former tutor in engineering at Edinburgh University. Fleeming had died on the 12th of that month: 'You know how much and for how long I have loved, respected, and admired him.... I never knew a better man nor one to me more lovable; we shall all feel the loss more greatly as time goes on'.

During Stevenson's time in Bournemouth, Scottish painter and engraver William Strang was commissioned by a London editor to visit him and produce an etching of him. When US painter John Singer Sargent painted Stevenson and his wife in August 1885, Sargent told novelist Henry James, 'Stevenson seemed to me the most intense creature I had ever met'. As for Stevenson, he described the occasion thus:

> Sargent was down again and painted a portrait of me walking about in my own dining-room, in my own velveteen jacket, and twisting as I go my own moustache: at one corner a glimpse of my wife, in an Indian dress, and seated in a chair that was once my grandfather's; but since some months goes by the name of Henry James's, for it was there the novelist loved to sit…

Stevenson goes on to say how, in the picture, his wife looks like 'a ghost', and refers, tongue-in-cheek, to his 'palatial entrance hall', and his 'respected staircase', which also feature in the painting. And finally, he says frankly of the work, 'All this is touched in lovely, with that witty touch of Sargent's; but, of course, it looks dam [n] queer as a whole'.

Sargent's depiction of Stevenson is poignant for two reasons: firstly, it shows him looking desperately thin and emaciated – typical features, for those suffering from chronic tuberculosis – secondly, it shows the interior of Skerryvore, a house which, as will shortly be seen, is no more. Sargent, subsequently, gave the work to, 'his friend' Stevenson, who hung it in the drawing room at Skerryvore.

On 28 October 1885, Stevenson in a letter to his father, cannot disguise, his delight that:

> …an illustrated TREASURE ISLAND will be out next month. I have an early copy and the French pictures [i.e. by French illustrator Georges Roux] are admirable… I would send you my copy BUT I CANNOT; it is my new toy and I cannot divorce myself from this enjoyment.

Skerryvore, from
the etching by
Leslie Ward.

On 26 December 1885, when he writes to W.H. Low, he is in a more serious mood:

> Mine is a strange contrivance; I don't die damme, and I cannot get along on both feet
> to save my soul; I am a chronic sickist; and my work cripples along between bed and the
> parlour, between the medicine bottle and the cupping glass [a hand-blown glass from which
> the air has been exhausted, which is applied to the skin and used to draw blood to the
> surface for letting].

But then, typically, he bounces back, saying, 'Well, I like my life all the same...'

On 2 January 1886 Stevenson tells Edmund Gosse, 'I do not write for the public; I do
write for money, a nobler deity; and most of all, for myself...' He also tells Gosse that he
does not believe 'in the immortality business,' but affirms that, 'we were put here to do
what service we can, for honour and not for hire...' He also discloses that he is working on
his *Memoir of Fleeming Jenkin*. On the 25th, he tells his father that he is working on *David
Balfour*, the sequel to *Kidnapped* (which was published in 1893).

Robert Louis Stevenson at Skerryvore, 1885.
Detail from painting by John Singer Sargent.
(Steve Wynn)

Fanny Stevenson at Skerryvore, 1885.
Detail from painting by John Singer Sargent.
(Steve Wynn)

In the autumn of 1886, Stevenson's parents rented a house in Bournemouth in order to be near their sick son. However, when his father's own health deteriorated his parents were obliged to return to Edinburgh, which they did the following April. In May 1887, Stevenson, even though he himself was far from well, was summoned to Edinburgh to the deathbed of his father.

In 1887, Stevenson published *The Merry Men and Other Tales and Fables*, which he dedicated to Sir Henry Taylor's wife, Theodosia:

My dear Lady Taylor,
  To your name, if I wrote on brass, I could add nothing; it has been already written higher than I could dream to reach, by a strong and clear hand; and if I now dedicate to you these tales, it is not as the writer who brings you his work, but as the friend who would remind you of his affection.
  Robert Louis Stevenson.[2]

Also in 1887, he published a volume of his poems entitled *Underwoods*, which he dedicated to Dr Thomas Bodley Scott, his physician and friend at Bournemouth (who subsequently became Mayor of the town). Describing physicians, in general, as, 'the flower (such as it is) of our civilization', he made specific mention of those who had attended him personally: Dr Willey of San Francisco, Karl Ruedi of Davos, Dr Herbert of Paris,

Frontispiece of the first edition of *Treasure Island*.

Dr Caissot of Montpellier, Dr Brandt of Royat, Dr Wakefield of Nice, Dr Chepmell, Dr Horace Dobell, Sir Andrew Clarke, and Stevenson's own uncle, Dr Balfour. The greatest praise, however, he reserved for Dr Bodley Scott. Said he: 'When my next misfortune brings him hurrying to me when he would fain sit down to meat, or lie down to rest, will he care to remember that he takes this trouble for one who is not fool enough to be ungrateful?'

Amongst the poems contained in *Underwoods* is one entitled, 'Skerryvore: a parallel':

Here, all is sunny, and when the truant gull
Skims the green level of the lawn, his wing
Dispetals roses; here the house is framed
Of kneaded brick and the plumed mountain pine,
Such clay as artists fashion and such wood
As the tree—climbing urchin breaks.

In August 1887, Stevenson sold Skerryvore and left Bournemouth, but before he did so, he asked the Taylors to scour London for a copy of Thomas Hardy's novel *The Woodlanders*, the only book that he wished to take with him on the voyage that was now before him.[3] On the 17th of that month, Stevenson sailed from London for New York with his wife, his mother and his stepson. The climate there, however, was not conducive to his health, and he relocated to the Aridondack Mountains in the northern part of New York State. Here, at Saranac Lake, he began his novel *The Master of Ballantrae*.

In June 1888, having crossed the continent, Stevenson and his entourage chartered the yacht *Casco* and on the 28th of that month sailed from San Francisco, across the Pacific Ocean to the Marquese Islands, Tahiti, Hawaii, the Gilbert Islands and Samoa, before finally arriving in Sydney, where illness again overtook him. He therefore returned to Samoa, believing that here in the tropics, the air would do him good.

In 1889, Stevenson purchased 314 acres of land on the slope of Mount Vaea, above Apia, capital of Samoa. Here, on the estate which he called 'Vailima' (Five Waters), he built a large mansion. In that year he published *The Master of Ballantrae*, which he dedicated to Sir Percy and Lady Shelley of Boscombe Manor. He wrote the 'Dedication' from Waikiki, Honolulu

…by the loud shores of a subtropical island near upon ten thousand miles from Boscombe Chine and Manor: scenes which rise before me as I write, along with the faces and voices of my friends'.

Well, I am for the sea once more [his next port of call was the Gilbert Islands;] no doubt Sir Percy also. Let us make the signal B.R.D!

R.L.S. Waikiki, May 17, 1889.

In Stevenson's time, flags were used for signalling between ships, 'BRD' being the international signalling code for 'adieu'. Stevenson may well have learned this in his younger days as a prospective lighthouse engineer.

In 1890, Stevenson's possessions – which were in store at Bournemouth – were sent on to him at Vailima. On hearing of the death of Lady Taylor, an event which occurred in January 1891, he wrote to her daughter Una:

What a good thing we are gone from Bournemouth. What would it be to us, now you [the Taylors] are gone? I have rarely liked a human being as I liked your mother: I admired, I relished, I loved her: admired her wit and the eternal beautiful evidences of her beauty; relished the devil that she had – it was a most familiar spirit; loved her for her high mind and her hot, impatient heart. It seems incredible that anything so vital should be gone from life. [4]

Stevenson died on 3 December 1894 at the age of forty-four, allegedly of a brain haemorrhage. He was buried, according to his wishes, on the slopes of Mount Vaea, overlooking Vailima.

On 15 November 1940, during the Second World War, Stevenson's former house in Bournemouth, Skerryvore, was damaged by a German bomb. The site was cleared, and in 1954, opened by Bournemouth Corporation as a memorial garden. Poet Edmund Gosse described how Stevenson's '…sympathy and sweetness, which radiated from all the features, precluded the faintest notion of want of sincerity'. It was difficult to believe, he said '…that the time will ever come in which Stevenson will not be remembered as the most beloved of the writers of that age which he did so much to cheer and stimulate by his example'.

24

Frederick W. Lacey

Frederick William Lacey, MICE, FRIBA, born in 1856, was Borough Engineer and Surveyor for Bournemouth from 1889 until the year of his death, 1916.

Having served as assistant to an eminent firm of architects in London, Lacey travelled to South America where he became resident engineer to a mining company. This involved him in constructing roads, aqueducts and bridges in the rugged terrain of the Andes Mountains. He subsequently travelled to Central America, the West Indies, the USA and Canada, where he took a particular interest in the architecture and layout of the towns and cities of those countries, before returning to his old firm in London. In 1889, having worked for eight years as surveyor to the local board in Brentford, Essex, he was appointed Engineer and Surveyor to Bournemouth Corporation.

Lacey oversaw the creation of Bournemouth's main drainage system, thirty miles of new street works, and extensive additions to the sanitary hospital. He also designed the town's East Cemetery at Pokesdown (1897), where two chapels were erected under one roof – one for the Church of England and the other for Nonconformists. However, Lacey regretted the fact that Bournemouth:

> …had no great public building, no noble monument, none of those things which make the habitation of men into that most wonderful of things – a home. For it is such monuments and graceful structures round which the childish fancy builds its airy places, round which in later days imagination flits and memory dwells.[1]

Therefore, following the example of his predecessors, Benjamin Ferrey, Decimus Burton, and Christopher Crabbe Creeke, Lacey became resolved to preside over the ongoing creation of a modern and beautiful town, and in this, he received the full support of Bournemouth's Mayor and corporation.

An example of the lengths to which Bournemouth's Council was prepared to go in order to ensure that the town's public buildings were to be not only fit for purpose but aesthetically pleasing to the eye, is indicated by a visit made by its committee to various parts of England over the course of ten days in the spring of 1900. This deputation, led by Deputy Mayor, Councillor Hoare, included F. W. Lacey, the Town Clerk, Alderman Mattocks, and Councillors Becket and Lawson.

In Birmingham, the committee observed that the new law courts were, 'of a much too elaborate and costly character for Bournemouth'. In Blackpool it noted that, 'the style and

Frederick William Lacey. (Reproduced with the kind permission of Russell-Cotes Art Gallery and Museum)

character' of the municipal offices, 'were not suited to Bournemouth'. In Bolton, however, they found a, 'well-designed Town Hall and municipal offices'. Rochdale, they said:

> …possesses a very handsome pile of municipal building, of high architectural merit, both in outward design and in the interior arrangements, decorations, and fittings… every detail having come under the notice of the architect, so that there was a striking harmony of design.

Other towns and cities visited included Oxford, Wakefield, Leeds, Sheffield, Croydon, Kingston-on-Thames, Chatham, Hastings, Eastbourne, and Leicester.[2]

It was Lacey who oversaw the creation of Bournemouth and District's tramway system. Prior to the tramway, those who could afford it were conveyed by horse-drawn vehicles, either in their own carriages, or by public omnibuses. Those who wished to venture farther afield could catch one of two, four-horsed coaches, which arrived at the Bath Hotel at two o'clock each afternoon – one from Southampton and one from Weymouth.[3]

The creation of tramways in Britain had been facilitated by the passing in 1870, of the 'Tramways Act', and of electric tramways by the 'Light Railways Act' of 1896. Under these Acts, the British Electric Traction Company Ltd., through its subsidiary the Poole and District Electric Traction Company Ltd, had built a tramway from Poole railway station to County Gates (via Ashley Road), which opened on 6 April 1901. (County Gates marked the boundary between Hampshire and Dorsetshire. Originally, a lodge with iron gates, it was situated at the

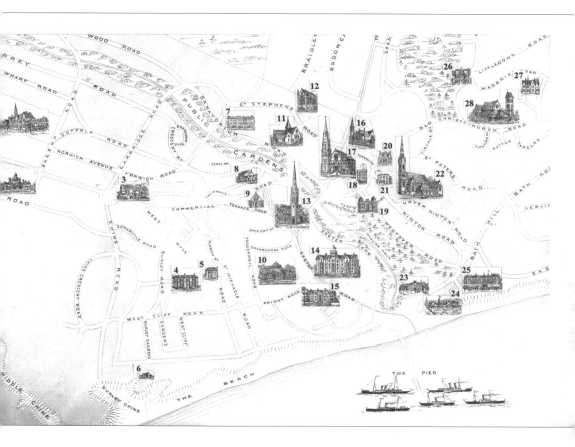

Principal buildings in Bournemouth in 1890 (after Garrett's Illustrated Map of Bournemouth):

1.	Bournemouth West Railway Station	16.	Roman Catholic Church
2.	Victoria Hospital	17.	Punshon Memorial Church
3.	St Michael's Church	18.	New Town Hall
4.	Hahnemann House	19.	Arcade
5.	Alexandra Hospital for Children	20.	Shaftesbury Hall and Gymnasium
6.	Sheltered Rustic Seat	21.	General Post Office
7.	National Sanatorium	22.	St Peter's Church
8.	Friends Meeting House	23.	Belle Vue and Pier Hotel
9.	Winter Gardens	24.	The Baths and Marlborough House
11.	Richmond Hill Congregational Church	25.	Royal Bath Hotel
12.	St Stephen's Church	26.	St Mary's Home
13.	St Andrew's Presbyterian Church	27.	Firs Home
14.	Royal Exeter Hotel	28.	Holy Trinity Church
15.	The Osborne		

(The Hotel Mont Dore is not shown, but was situated adjacent to the National Sanatorium.)

northern end of The Avenue – a private road leading to Branksome Tower). In 1902, the Poole and District Electric Traction Company was bought out by Poole Council, which leased it to Bournemouth Corporation for a period of thirty years.

A truly prodigious programme of tramway construction was now undertaken, so that in the years 1902 to 1906, Pokesdown, Winton, Moordown, Lower Parkstone, Westbourne, Boscombe, Southbourne and Christchurch were all linked to the Poole system (the first tramcar from Poole to Bournemouth running on 3 July 1905, and the first from Poole to Christchurch Priory on 17 October of that year).

In August 1904, Bournemouth Town Council instructed Lacey to prepare a scheme for an under-cliff drive and sea wall. This was opened on 6 November 1907, and extended eastwards from the pier for a distance of 760 yards, to just below the end of Meyrick Road.

On 17 February 1906, a report was published, 'on Sketch design "E"' for the proposed new Bournemouth Municipal Buildings, Law Courts and Town Hall. As already indicated, great care was to be taken with regard to their architectural appearance: it being noted that, 'the traditional style of English Renaissance is now generally followed in all building[s] of a similar character…'. As for the 'so-called Jacobean style', this was now considered to be obsolete.

Architects F.W. Lacey and C.E. Mallows, who had jointly prepared the scheme which was presently under consideration, declared that this was, 'the fifth complete one we have made', all five of which were, 'the outcome of some hundreds of drawings and sketches, including block plans showing the general arrangement upon the site'.[4] The Law Courts, in Stafford Road, which Lacey designed in conjunction with H.A. Collins, opened in 1914. With regard to the municipal buildings and Town Hall, however, Lacey's efforts came to nought, and, as already mentioned, the Hotel Mont Dore eventually became the Town Hall.

Lacey also designed the Central Fire Station (Holdenhurst Road, 1902) and the College and Public Library (Christchurch Road, 1913). He also oversaw the installation of electric lighting in the pleasure grounds, the creation of the Winter Gardens (designed by architects Messrs Fletcher, Lowndes & Co. of London, which opened in 1877), and the construction of Bournemouth's first iron pier, designed by Eugenius Birch and built in 1880, complete with clock tower, tea house, pier-head kiosk and bandstand.

By the early 1880s, the commoners of the Bournemouth region had virtually ceased to exercise their rights of turbary – the cutting of turf for use as fuel – on the five plots of land held in trust by Sir George Meyrick (3rd Baronet) under the terms of the Christchurch Enclosure Act of 1802. Therefore, in 1889, the Bournemouth Park Lands Act was passed by Parliament, authorizing the use of these plots of land as 'open spaces for the recreation and enjoyment of the public under the exclusive regulation and management of the Commissioners'.

Of these five plots, 'Allotment No. 62', known as 'Poor's Common', lay between Talbot Woods and the town centre. 126½ acres in size, it was bisected by the railway line – constructed in 1884-85 – linking Bournemouth's East and West Stations. However, when Sir George Meyrick donated the southern portion of this Allotment to Bournemouth Corporation (at no charge), F.W. Lacey was able to earmark it for what would become 'Meyrick Park'.

One of the features of this 118-acre park was an eighteen-hole golf course, the first municipally planned golf links in the country, which was laid out by Scotsman Thomas

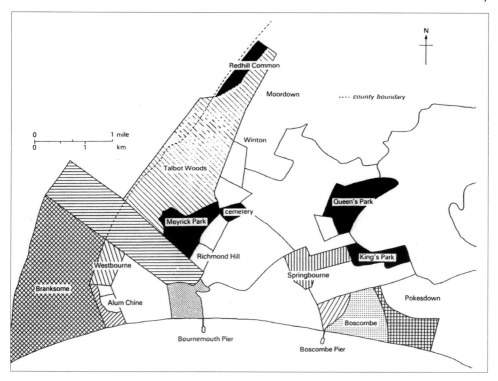

Location of Bournemouth's Parks and Wimborne Road Cemetery.

Dunn, golf club manufacturer and golf course architect. It also contained three cricket grounds, two football grounds, two hockey pitches and six bowling greens, each with their own pavilion. Meyrick Park was opened on 28 November 1894 by Jacintha, wife of Sir George A.E.T.G. Meyrick, 4th Baronet. Subsequently, following a donation of seventy-six acres of land from the Talbot Estate by the Earl of Leven and Melville, the size of Meyrick Park was increased to 194 acres.

Under the terms of the Bournemouth Corporation Act of 1900, all commoners' rights over the remaining plots of land were abolished, and in April, Bournemouth Corporation acquired sixty-four acres of 'Allotment No. 59' from Meyrick. This became King's Park, which opened on 21 June 1902. It subsequently boasted a cricket ground and pavilion, bowling greens and an athletic centre. (King's Park subsequently increased in size to 86½ acres).

The 147½ acres of 'Allotment No. 60', which Bournemouth Corporation also acquired from Meyrick, became Queen's Park, which opened in 1902. On 25 October 1905, its golf links, laid out by John Henry ('JH') Taylor, four-times Open champion, was opened by Alderman J.E. Beale. The final size of Queen's Park was 173 acres. Of the two remaining plots, one became Redhill Common.

Lacey was also involved with the laying out and landscaping of Durley and Alum Chines (including the erection of bridges over the chines), the East and West Cliffs, and the West Overcliff Drive.

Lower Pleasure Gardens, *c.* 1900. (Fraser Donachie)

Lacey died at his home, 'Alum Chine Lodge', on 24 March 1916, aged sixty. In appreciation of his twenty-seven years of service as Borough Engineer for the town, a special meeting of the Council was convened on 4 April, where it was resolved that a 'Resolution' be engraved on vellum, framed, and hung in the Council Chamber.

From the mid-1930s, trolleybuses began to replace the tram service, which came to an end on 8 April 1936, when the service from Bournemouth Square to Christchurch was finally closed.

25

Sir Winston Churchill

The Bournemouth/Poole area, together with the Isle of Wight, are the only places in Britain where there are 'chines', and it was at one of these chines, in 1893, that future British Prime Minister and wartime leader, Winston Leonard Spencer Churchill, almost came to a premature end!

Whilst a pupil at Harrow School, Winston sat the entrance examinations for the Royal Military Academy, Sandhurst. Having failed for the second time, it was arranged that he should go to a Captain James at Cromwell Road, London, who presided over, 'a crammer which specialized in preparing boys for the examination'. Before his studies began, however, he, his mother Lady Churchill, his brother John, and a cousin visited Bournemouth. Here, as was their custom in the winter months, they stayed with Cornelia Guest, sister of Winston's father, Lord Randolph Churchill. Cornelia was the first Lady Wimborne, and her home was Canford Magna, near Wimborne in Dorset. However, she also owned a Victorian seaside villa, 'Branksome Dene', at Alum Chine, Bournemouth, together with forty acres or so of pine forest. Winston himself sets the scene, the date being the afternoon of 10 January 1893:

> I was 18 and on my holiday. My younger brother [Jack] aged 12, and a cousin [Ivor] aged 14, proposed to chase me. After I had been hunted for 20 minutes and was rather short of breath, I decided to cross the bridge [over the chine]. Arrived at its centre, I saw to my consternation that the pursuers had divided their forces. One stood at each end of the bridge; capture seemed certain. But in a flash there came across me a great project.

The 'project' which Winston had in mind was to leap off the bridge and clutch at the branches of some young fir trees as he descended. This, he hoped, would break his fall:

> My young pursuers stood wonderstruck at either end of the bridge. To plunge or not to plunge that was the question! In a second I had plunged, throwing out my arms to embrace the summit of the fir tree… It was three days before I regained consciousness and more than three months before I crawled from my bed. The measured fall was 29 feet onto hard ground.

Winston's companions rushed to his mother and told her, 'He jumped over the bridge and he won't speak to us'. Lady Churchill's thoughts may only be imagined. His father returned post haste from Ireland, bringing 'the greatest of London surgeons with him'.

Winston Churchill as a schoolboy at Harrow School. (Reproduced by permission of the Harrow School Archive)

Amongst Winston's other injuries was a ruptured kidney. Said he, subsequently, 'It is to the surgeon's art and to my own pronounced will-to-live that the reader is indebted for this story'.[1]

Winston would revisit the area on 17 July 1940, during the Second World War, in order to inspect the sea defenses that were being prepared in the event of 'Operation Sea Lion', Adolf Hitler's planned invasion of Britain, coming to fruition.

On 7 August 2007, an article by Darren Slade appeared in the *Bournemouth Echo*. He had deduced, from a perusal of old Ordnance Survey maps, that the bridge which Winston jumped from, was the 'rustic bridge… at Branksome Dene Chine, near the home of his aunt, Lady Wimborne'. This bridge no longer exists.

26

Guglielmo Marconi

Guglielmo Marconi, who arrived in England in 1896, experimented in wireless telegraphy from a house near the seafront of Bournemouth in January 1898.

Marconi was born on 25 April 1874 in Bologna, Italy, of a wealthy Italian father and an Irish mother. He was educated first by private tutors and subsequently at the Istituto Cavallero in Florence, at Bologna University under Professor of Physics Augusto Righi, and at Livorno under Physics Professor Giotto Bizzarrini. (At the latter place, he was also taught privately by Physics Professor Vincenzo Rosa of the Liceo Nicolini). In Righi's laboratory, Marconi acquired a knowledge of oscillators (transmitters) and resonators (receivers), as used by German physicist Heinrich Hertz (who in 1887 was the first to give a satisfactory demonstration of the existence of 'Hertzian' waves – now known as radio waves – and also to demonstrate how they could be both transmitted and detected. However, as yet, no one had managed to transmit a signal a distance of more than about 100 yds).

It fell to the youthful Marconi to achieve this breakthrough, which he did, using 'home-made equipment [and] an elevated aerial, and earthing his transmitter and receiver'.[1] Marconi conducted his first experiments in the granary at his home Villa Griffone, Pontecchio, near Bologna, which he converted into a laboratory. His aim was to create a practical system of wireless telegraphy (i.e. one which did not depend on connecting wires, such as were used in the electric telegraph). In the spring of 1895 he succeeded in transmitting signals from his garden to a barn a mile or so away, even though the barn was hidden behind a hill.

Having had his proposals for a system of wireless communication rejected by the Ministry of Posts and Telegraphy in Rome, the twenty-two-year-old Marconi travelled to England, arriving in London with his apparatus, on 2 February 1896. Having attracted the interest and support of William Preece, Chief Engineer to the British Post Office, he continued with his experiments, both in the capital and on Salisbury Plain, Wiltshire (in the presence of experts from the British Army and Navy). On 2 June 1896, he was granted the first British patent for wireless telegraphy.

On 13 May 1897, Marconi sent the first ever wireless signal across the open sea – a distance of nine miles across the Bristol Channel. That summer, 1897, he returned to his home country, where, at La Spezia on the coast of north-west Italy, he demonstrated his work to the Italian Navy. However, even now, he failed to gain the support of the Italian government.

On 20 July 1897, Marconi established the Wireless Telegraph and Signal Company. In the summer of 1898, he transmitted messages from Osborne House – Queen Victoria's

Madeira Hotel.

Guglielmo Marconi.

royal residence on the Isle of Wight – to the royal yacht *Osborne*. On 27 March 1899, he sent the first message (in Morse code) across the English Channel from South Foreland, St Margaret's Bay, Dover, Kent, to Wimereux, a coastal town near Boulogne. In the same year in the USA, he transmitted reports of the America's Cup yacht races from the liner *Ponce* to the mainland, and proceeded to establish a wireless telegraphy company in America, just as he had done in Britain.

In November 1897, Marconi set up a wireless transmitting station on the cliffs at Alum Bay on the Isle of Wight. Four months later he established a second station at the Madeira Hotel, near Bournemouth Pier. Here, in the front garden, he erected an aerial and set up a laboratory in an underground cellar. Subsequently having fallen out with the management of the hotel (whose proprietress was a Mrs Jolliffe), he moved his equipment to the house next door, 'Sandhills', in the garden of which he erected a 125ft-high mast in order to exchange messages with his Isle of Wight station, and with ships at sea.

In a letter to the *Bournemouth Daily Echo*,[2] Percy Newlyn declared:

These experiments were then, more or less, secret and were conducted between here [Bournemouth] and The Needles [Isle of Wight], but the point which gives Bournemouth the claim to priority in regard to them is that it was between these two points that he achieved the first fulfillment of his dreams, i.e. a 2-way communication.

I well remember the day on which the 2-way communication was achieved, as the man who held the purse strings [believed to be Scottish physicist and mathematician Lord Kelvin] was residing in the Royal Exeter Hotel, and a private luncheon to celebrate the occasion was held by those few intimately concerned.[3]

In another letter to the *Bournemouth Daily Echo* dated 4 May 1940, F.A. Olding of Moordown wrote that he too could:

…well remember the day on which the 2-way communication was made, since I was privileged to see something of the delight with which the inventor declared his triumph on that occasion. On a warm, sunny afternoon, early in the season I think, I walked up the Bournemouth Pier with a message from my mother to her cousin, Capt. Cox of the SS Victoria, just as that vessel was berthing.

I was startled to see a slight, dark man in a blue suit, dash excitedly up the gangway, waving his right hand to the piermaster on the upper deck and shouting, 'I've done it – I've done it.' With a small black box tucked under his left arm he continued a run down the pier shouting, 'I've done it,' as he went.

Madeira Hotel, Bournemouth (the building on the right of the photograph). (Bournemouth Library)

Going on board, I soon enquired from the captain the reason for the excitement, and was told that the man was an Italian named Marconi, and that he had told the captain that the 'box' he had under his arm had enabled him that day to send, as well as receive signals by 'wireless', and that it was the first time that it had been done in this way. Previously, he had been able to receive only on the island [of Wight], and not send.

It was on 3 June 1898, that 'Sandhills' had the honour of receiving the world's first, paid 'radiogram' – transmitted from the Isle of Wight by Marconi on behalf of Lord Kelvin (who insisted on paying a shilling for each message of greeting he sent to his friends, who had assembled on Marconi's cliff-top station in Bournemouth).[4]

W. Lloyd Woodland describes how, during his time as a journalist in Bournemouth, he was proud of the fact:

…that I am one of the very few who were privileged to be present at Marconi's first Press demonstration of his great discovery. My seniors thought the occasion of so little moment that they sent me, the youngest member of the staff, to 'see what that foreigner has been playing about with on the West Cliff.'

I shall never forget that afternoon and my excitement when the long electric flashes from the 'sender' at one end of the Old Shaftesbury Hall, evoked responses from the copper-winged receivers on the platform at the opposite end of the hall; and how we were shown the working of the 'cohearer' – two terminals in a glass tube, spaced slightly apart, with silver filings in the gap. Wireless worked before our eyes; we could see the tiny silver particles jump together each time the 'sender' flashed.[5]

In 1900, Marconi changed the name of his enterprise to the 'Marconi Wireless Telegraph Company'. On 16 October 1902, a reporter from The Bournemouth Graphic declared:

Signor Marconi is not, by any means, easy to catch. That he is a busy man goes without saying, but he is more than that – he is a scientist, so engrossed with his researches in the marvellous realms of science, that he thinks little and cares less about publicity or self-advertisement.

In September 1898, Marconi transferred his headquarters to The Haven Hotel (formerly the Haven Coaching Inn), Sandbanks, Poole, where he again built a laboratory and erected an aerial.

The sending by Marconi on 12 December 1901 of the first transatlantic message, from Poldhu, Cornwall to Signal Hill, St John's, Newfoundland, a distance of over 2,000 miles, was the crowning moment of his career. This was despite the fact that scientists believed that wireless signals would be lost after 165 miles, due to the curvature of the Earth. He was then aged only twenty-seven.

In March 1905, Marconi married Beatrice, daughter of Irishman Edward Donough O'Brien, 14th Baron Inchiquin. In 1909, he was awarded the Nobel Prize for Physics (sharing it with German physicist Karl Ferdinand Braun, inventor of the cathode ray oscillator). In 1912, thanks to Marconi, the stricken liner RMS Titanic was able to send out a distress signal, which enabled over 700 of her 2,300 passengers and crew to be rescued.

Guglielmo Marconi in his laboratory at the Madeira Hotel, Bournemouth. (Court Royal, Bournemouth)

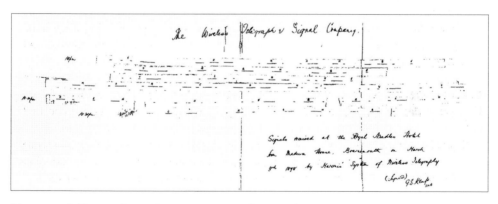

Message reads 'Orange Orange Love Marconi Hurrah Orange'. (Court Royal, Bournemouth)

In 1914, Marconi was appointed Honorary Knight Grand Cross of the Royal Victorian Order. The following year his company began using continuous-wave transmitters, which enabled the Marconi factory at Chelmsford, Essex, to transmit the United Kingdom's first radio entertainment broadcasts. In 1924, Marconi was made Marchese (Marquis) by Italian King Victor Emmanuel III. In 1927, on behalf of the British government, he created a radio telegraph network across the British Empire.

Marconi died in Rome on 20 July 1937, aged sixty-three; news of his death being transmitted by wireless communication throughout the world, with radio stations closing down for two minutes as a mark of respect. He was honoured with a state funeral.

In 1947, Bournemouth's Madeira Hotel became the Court Royal, a convalescent home for South Wales miners.

Flora Thompson

Bournemouth was where Flora Thompson came to live in 1903, and where she spent more than a decade during her formative years as a writer.

Flora Jane Timms, author of *Lark Rise to Candleford*, was born on 5 December 1876 at Juniper Hill, a tiny hamlet of thatched cottages near Cottisford in Oxfordshire. She was the eldest of the six surviving children of Albert, a stonemason, and his wife Emma, daughter of a smallholder, and nursemaid to the children of a local curate. Flora attended her village school and, in her spare time, roamed the countryside – which was her greatest pleasure – in the company of her younger brother, Edwin.

Having left school at fourteen, Flora started work at the Post Office at Fringford, near Bicester, in Oxfordshire, as assistant to postmistress Mrs Kezia Whitton. The postmistress duly took her young charge under her wing, and helped her to become proficient in such subjects as arithmetic and geography. Flora left Fringford in 1897 and worked at several different locations, including a Post Office in London, where the nearest available 'countryside' was Kew Gardens.

Flora was working as a clerk at Twickenham Post Office when she met John Thompson, also a Post Office clerk. The couple were married on 7 January 1903 at the Parish Church of St Mary the Virgin, Twickenham. Shortly afterwards, they moved to the rapidly expanding village of Winton, on the northern outskirts of Bournemouth, where John would take up a position as sorting clerk and telegraphist at Bournemouth's main Post Office. Flora was now obliged to give up work as the Post Office did not employ married women. Among the addresses in Winton where the couple lived were Number 4 (and subsequently Number 6), Sedgley Road, Grayshott Cottage in Edgehill Road (Grayshott being the name of the Hampshire village where Flora had lived and worked from 1898 to 1901) and Frederica Road (where they again called their house Grayshott Cottage).

Winton was surrounded by pine woods and heathland, where Flora enjoyed walking. One of her favourite walks was to nearby Talbot Village – created, as already mentioned, by sisters Georgina and Mary Talbot. Attractive as this 'model village' was, Flora was painfully aware that this was a time of rapid development, where the countryside was quickly being gobbled up by new housing estates. Flora also enjoyed walking to Skerryvore, Robert Louis Stevenson's former house in Westbourne; her admiration for the Scottish writer being revealed by her in the following lines:

Skerryvore stands just as he left it. Memorial tablets to his pet dog bear witness to his love for all living creatures. In their season, rhododendron blooms make vivid splashes of colour

Flora Thompson
and son Henry in
1911. (Norman
Phillips)

against the dark pines that once delighted his artist soul. From the upper windows may still be
seen a glimpse of the sea that he delighted to point out to his guests. Only he, the life and soul
of it all, has gone.[1]

In autumn 1903, Flora's first child, Winifred Grace, was born. Now, writing must take
second place:

> With a house to run single-handed; with children being born and nursed, my literary dreams
> faded for a while but I still read a good deal. For the first time in my life I had access to a good
> library, and I slipped in like a duck slipping into water and read almost everything.[2]

It was only when she arrived in Bournemouth, said Flora, that 'her real education' began.
The library to which Flora referred was Bournemouth's first public library, which
was opened on 1 January 1895 by the Mayor, Sir Merton Russell-Cotes in temporary

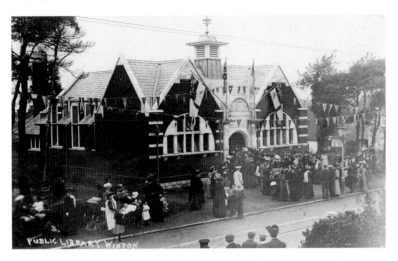

The opening of Winton Library in 1907. (Reproduced by permission of Bournemouth Libraries)

premises at 6, Cumnor Terrace, Old Christchurch Road (together with a reading room at Boscombe). This was made possible by the Public Libraries Act of 1892, which provided a legal framework whereby such public facilities might be established. In 1903, a Libraries Committee was created, and in June 1894, Charles Riddle was appointed Bournemouth's first Borough Librarian.

The library at Cumnor Terrace was unique in the area, in that it offered 'open access' – i.e. books were put out on the shelves for readers to see, whereas the custom of the time was that the reader had to know, in advance, the name of the book that he or she required, in order to request it from the librarian. In introducing 'open access', Bournemouth Library was emulating London's Clerkenwell Public Library, which had been the first to introduce the system in May 1894. In 1898, travelling libraries began supplying books to residents throughout the borough, and the following year, branch libraries were established at Boscombe, Springbourne and Westbourne.

Subsequently, on 21 October 1901, the Cumnor Terrace Library relocated to improved accommodation at 2 Stanhope Gardens, Dean Park Road (until finally, on 26 March 1913, a permanent site for Bournemouth's Central Library was found at the Lansdowne). Said Flora, 'the public library there was my alma mater. I had no guide and it was better so. The discovery of each new writer, each set of new ideas, was the opening up of a new world'.

She read works by the Greeks and Romans (in translation), the English poets, novelists and critics, translations of French writers and 'even tried my teeth upon philosophy and mysticism!' Soon, Winton was to have a library of its own, which would obviate the need for her to walk to Bournemouth. As the plaque on the wall of Winton Library states:

This library, the gift of Andrew Carnegie, Esq. LLD [Scottish industrialist, businessman, and major philanthropist], is erected on land presented by the eleventh Earl of Leven and Melville and was opened by Alderman JA Parsons JP, Mayor of Bournemouth, on 26th day of October 1907.

For Flora, this was manna from heaven! Her second child, Henry Basil, was born on 6 October 1909. In 1910, she began to subscribe to a one-penny magazine called *The Ladies Companion* which, in February 1911, held a competition for the best 300-word essay on Jane Austen. Flora entered, and won first prize – a book, or books, to the value of 5s. She went on to win prizes for essays on Emily Brontë and the Shakespearian heroine 'Juliette'.

Flora's great joy was to travel by train with her children to the New Forest, which she describes as a 'wonderland', and which features in her short story *His Lady of the Lilacs*:

> He steps from the primitive platform through a wicket gate, and the green peace of the forest closed upon him. There was no other building in site, the road to the village wound between banks where the last primroses lingered with the first bluebells.[3]

In January 1912, *The Ladies Companion* printed Flora's short story 'The Toft Club' – a romance set in the New Forest in wintertime. This was the first occasion, but not the last, that she would receive payment for her work. Many more of her stories would be published in magazines in the years to come, and the fees thereby accrued would make a welcome supplement to the Thompson family's meager income. When Flora persuaded her husband John, to buy her a typewriter, she was now able to type out not only the minutes of his Postal Clerk's Association Meetings, but also her own entries for magazine competitions.

When, on 14 April 1912, the White Star liner RMS *Titanic* sank after striking an iceberg – with the loss of 1,513 lives – Scottish physician and writer Ronald Campbell Macfie, wrote an ode on the sinking. It was published in the magazine *Literary Monthly*, which held a competition in which readers were invited to submit criticisms of the ode. Flora did so, and again, won first prize. Macfie was in no way put out by Flora's criticism; instead he expressed his appreciation of it by visiting her in Bournemouth, whereupon they struck up a friendship. A specialist in the treatment of tuberculosis, and author of books on medicine, hygiene, and evolution, Macfie, as a poet himself, encouraged Flora in her own desire to write poetry. She responded by writing this poem for him:

> Yours are the moors, the billowy seas,
> Tall mountains and blue distances.
> Mine is a cottage garden, set
> With marigold and mignonette,
> And all the wildling things that dare,
> Without a gardener's fostering care.
> Yet very well-content I rest
> In my obscure, sequestered nest:
> Far from my cottage garden I
> Can see your cloud-peaks pierce the sky!

During her time in Bournemouth, Flora attended meetings of the Women's Suffrage Movement which campaigned for votes for women. Her view was that the vote, once secured for her sex, would make women the equals of men in terms of prestige and opportunity.[4]

The First World War commenced in August 1914. On 26 April 1916, Flora's younger brother Edwin – of the Eastern Ontario Regiment – whom she described as 'the companion of my childhood', was killed in action in Belgium. In August 1916, Flora's time in Bournemouth came to an end when her husband John, was appointed sub-postmaster at Liphook in Hampshire.

Flora once said 'Leisure, that priceless boon, which all my life has been denied me, is necessary before I can attempt great things'. In other words, the bringing up of her children (she had another child, Peter Redmond Thompson in 1918), and her work at the Post Office, left little time for her great passion in life, which was writing. This is, perhaps, why she did not write her first major work until she was aged sixty-two.

Nevertheless, when Ronald Campbell Macfie encouraged Flora to submit a collection of her poems for publication, the outcome was that her *Bog Myrtle and Peat* was published in 1921 by Philip Allen & Co.

Given the fact that both Flora and her husband were employees of the Post Office, it is not surprising that *Lark Rise to Candleford*, first published in 1945, features a heroine 'Laura', who finds a position at Candleford Post Office. The novel was, in fact, a trilogy of semi-autobiographical works, which included *Lark Rise* (published in 1939), *Over to Candleford* (1941), and *Candleford Green* (1943). The story, set in an obscure Oxfordshire village in the late nineteenth century, depicts rural life as seen through the eyes of teenager 'Laura Timmins'. The fictitious hamlet of 'Lark Rise' – so called because of the abundance of skylarks in its surrounding fields – is, in reality, Juniper Hill in Oxfordshire where Flora grew up. 'Candleford' was its wealthier neighbour.

Lark Rise to Candleford is more than simply a tale of village life. It describes a period of enormous change, where centuries-old rural traditions are being swept away in the name of 'progress'. With the Enclosure Acts, the countryside is being carved up, and the labourers forced off the land, which they have inhabited, worked, and enjoyed for centuries. Cottages are being replaced with modern villas; the ancient skills – that of the ploughman, the wheelwright, the cobbler, and so forth – are no longer required, and machines take over. New and noisy railways disturb the tranquility, and an increasingly inflexible bureaucracy begins to govern the lives of ordinary people. And the result? That priceless amenity, the countryside, with its woods and streams, meadows and wild flowers, begins to vanish forever.

A sequel to *Lark Rise to Candleford*, entitled *Still Glides the Stream*, appeared in 1948. Sadly, Flora did not live to see it published. She died at Brixham, Devon, on 21 May 1947, and is buried at Longcross Cemetery, Dartmouth.

D.H. Lawrence

When English poet, novelist, and essayist David Herbert Lawrence arrived in Bournemouth on 7 January 1912, he was at something of a crossroads in his life. His mother Lydia, to whom he was emotionally very close, had died on 9 December 1910; he himself was in indifferent health, and in the third week of November 1911, he became seriously ill. In addition, his relationship with his fiancée, Louisa Burrows, was deteriorating.

Born at Eastwood, Nottingham, on 11 September 1885, Lawrence was the fourth child (of five) of Arthur John Lawrence, a coal mine employee and his wife Lydia (née Beardsall), a qualified teacher. Lawrence attended Nottingham High School, to which he had won a scholarship. He had known Louisa – whom he called 'Louie' – since about 1900. From 1902, they had both attended the teacher training centre at Ilkeston, Derbyshire, from where they progressed, in 1906, to University College, Nottingham. In their second and final year, both Lawrence and Louisa 'were placed in the first class on their performance in the examinations for the Teacher's Certificate'.[1]

In October 1908, Lawrence was appointed teacher at the Davidson Road School in Croydon, Surrey. As for Louisa, she found a teaching post in Leicester and subsequently, on 1 January 1909, became headmistress of the village school at Ratcliffe-on-the-Wreke, four miles from Quorn. In that year, a number of Lawrence's poems were published in *The English Review*. On 3 December 1910, Lawrence asked Louisa to marry him; she accepted. In 1911, Lawrence's first novel, *The White Peacock*, was published by William Heinemann.

In the third week of November 1911, Lawrence contracted pneumonia with the 'crisis in the illness coming on about the 29th of that month'.[2] (His pneumonia was probably precipitated by underlying tuberculosis – even though tests of his sputum proved negative). He was nursed by his sister Ada. On 7 December he wrote to Louisa from his home, 16 Colworth Road, Addiscombe, on the outskirts of Croydon, 'My Dear Lou… I think the doctor [believed to be a Dr Addey] will let me go to Bournemouth, or somewhere, for the New Year. Will you come for the week?'[3] Two days later, he wrote to Louisa again, 'It is great news, is it not, that we may go straight to Bournemouth in a fortnight… There are pine trees at Bournemouth, pine woods, and the warm sea, and it is only a fortnight [to wait].'[4] And after another two days, he wrote, 'Christmas will soon be here – & I shall be getting up. The yellow jasmine is so bonnie. I kiss you with love'.[5]

In the event, Louisa did not join Lawrence in Bournemouth. However, she did stay with him at Addiscombe during the last week of December 1911. On 18 December, Lawrence wrote to his friend Edward Garnett, writer, critic, and reader for London publishers

D.H. Lawrence, 1912.

Duckworth & Co., indicating that his financial position was far from secure:

If you offer the thing [a story for publication] to Duckworth, do not, I beg you, ask for an advance on royalties. Do not present me as a beggar. Do not tell him I am poor. Heinemann owes me £50 in February – I have enough money to tide me over till he pays – and the fifty [pounds] will, at home, last me six months.[6]

On 30 December 1911, he told Garnett:

I am to go to Bournemouth – Lord, how sick I am of this ordering and countermanding [presumably by his doctors] – I loathe to be an invalid… I hate to be waited on. If ever I am ill again I shall die of mortification.[7]

When he arrived in Bournemouth on 7 January 1912, he wrote again to Garnett, to complain about Compton House, St Peter's Road, where he was staying:

I don't like it very much. It's a sort of go-as-you-please boarding-house, where I shall be far more alone than if I had gone into apartments, as I wanted to do. I think I get a bit impatient of people. But there, one is always churlish after an illness. When I'm better tempered I shall like the old maids and the philistine men and the very proper and proprietous maidens right enough. It is always raining – so stupid of it.[8]

Clearly, Lawrence found the atmosphere of Bournemouth somewhat starchy. However, by the following day, when he wrote to Louisa, he was in a better frame of mind, describing Compton House as:

… a jolly place – you would like it… There are 45 people in [residence] all sorts. One gets up at 8.30 & breakfasts at 9 – very prolific breakfast – bacon & kidney & ham & eggs – what you like. I chatter in the smoke-room until about 10.30 – then work in my room (where I have a fire made) – until 1.30 when we have lunch… In the afternoon I go out, or if it's wet, like today, I just stop in the recreation room & we play cards & games… I get such a lot better – the air suits me'.

As for the town of Bournemouth, Lawrence described it as:

… very pretty. When you look back at it, it's quite dark green with trees. There is a great bay & long, smashing waves, always close to the prom., [promenade] because there are four tides a day. At night, with the full moon along the surf & the foam smashing up, it is lovely.[9]

On 12 January 1912, Lawrence told Louisa of, 'a big fog' which came in from over the sea the previous day:

It is a peculiar colour this sea – either milk white, or a very pale, pure stone-colour, or a dove grey: so pale and ghostly, with opalescent tints. I admire it. I admire it very much.

This, however, is at variance with what Lawrence told his childhood sweetheart Jessica Chambers:

I advise you never to come here for a holiday… It's like a huge hospital. At every turn you come across invalids being pushed or pulled along. I shall be glad when I get away.[10]

On 17 January 1912, Lawrence was again admiring the 'beautiful rough sea'. He told Louisa that he had paid visits to Christchurch, and also to Poole Harbour. This would be followed by visits to Branksome Chine, Poole and Wimborne.

During his time in Bournemouth, Lawrence was not idle. He rewrote *The Saga of Siegmund*, and prepared it for publication under a new title, *The Trespasser* (published in 1912). This is the story of violin teacher Siegmund MacNair, who feels that he cannot desert his wife and family for his former pupil Helena Verden, who in turn feels that she cannot give herself completely to him. Here, he was reflecting, to a degree, turmoil in his own love life, for he was beginning to have serious doubts about Louisa.

By the end of January 1912, when he was about to leave Bournemouth, Lawrence's health was much improved, and he was feeling more cheerful. Said he, 'I can walk quite well. I can do six miles by now'.[11] However, his doctor in Bournemouth advised him to retire from teaching on health grounds, and devote himself henceforth to his writing.

On 3 February 1912, Lawrence left Bournemouth and spent a few days with Garnett at his home, 'The Cearne', near Edenbridge, Kent. From here, he wrote to Louisa to tell her what was on his mind:

You'll be wondering why I am so long in writing. I have been thinking what the doctor at Croydon & the doctor at Bournemouth both urged on me: that I ought not to marry, at least for a long time, if ever. And I feel myself my health is so precarious, I wouldn't undertake the responsibility. Then, seeing I mustn't teach, I shall have a struggle to keep myself… [And he ends the letter] It is no good to go on. I asked Ada [his sister] and she thought it would be better if the engagement were broken off; because it is not fair to you. It's a miserable business, and the fault is all mine.[12]

Four days later, he wrote again to Louisa:

…I do really feel it would be better to break the engagement. I don't think now I have the proper love to marry on. Have you not felt it so?[13]

The winter of 1911/12 was therefore a time of crisis in Lawrence's life, not only for health reasons, but also in regard to his career and personal relationships.

There are further echoes of Lawrence's own life in his novel *Sons and Lovers*, which he wrote during the time that he was courting Louisa Burrows. For example, the hero of the story, Paul Morel, comes from a coal mining family, and his lady friend Miriam Leiver's sister, Agatha, is a schoolteacher. On a deeper level, through Paul Morel, Lawrence reveals his own dilemma, when the former tells Miriam, 'I can only give friendship – It's all I'm capable of – It's a flaw in my make-up… I don't think I love you as a man ought to love his wife… I don't think one person would ever monopolize me – be everything to me.' Finally, Miriam asks of him, 'What do you want Paul?'[14] Clara Dawes, with whom Paul has an affair and who is also dissatisfied, says to him accusingly '…you've never given me yourself…you've never come near to me…you've given me everything, except yourself.'[15] Paul attributes his failure to commit to a woman to his relationship with his mother: 'There was one place in the world that stood solid and did not melt into unreality: the place where his mother was… It was as if the pivot and pole of his life, from which he could not escape, was his mother'. [16]

Daughters of the Vicar was another work which Lawrence was writing at the time when he was courting Louisa, and again, it deals with inter-personal relationships, and the ability, or otherwise, of a man or a woman to love and be loved. He wrote several other novels, including *The Rainbow* (1915) and *Lady Chatterley's Lover* (1928), which in those days caused a sensation as it was considered to be obscene. He also wrote essays, and several volumes of poetry.

Shortly after he broke off his engagement to Louisa, Lawrence met Frieda Weekley (née von Richthoven), daughter of a German baron and wife of Ernest Weekley, his former Professor of Modern Languages at the University of Nottingham. He married her on 13 July 1914, after her divorce.

The couple travelled to Germany, Austria, France, and Italy, and they lived for a time in Ceylon, Australia and New Mexico. This was in an effort to discover a climate which would suit Lawrence's health. It was in vain, and in 1924, in Mexico City, he had his first major pulmonary haemorrhage, after which an x-ray confirmed the fact that he was indeed suffering from tuberculosis, and that it was at an advanced stage.

On his last visit to Germany in 1929, when he knew that he was dying, Lawrence wrote his poem entitled 'The Ship of Death':

> Now it is autumn and the falling fruit
> And the long journey toward oblivion…

The first vaccine for tuberculosis was developed in the early years of the twentieth century at the Pasteur Institute in Lille, by French bacteriologists Albert Calmette and Camille Guérin – hence the vaccine's name, BCG (Bacillus of Calmette and Guérin). The vaccine was first used on human beings in France in 1921. However, mass vaccination of populations did not occur until after the Second World War. (Even then, although this was a huge step forward, the vaccine was not always 100 per cent effective).

For those already infected by tuberculosis, it was not until 1943, with the discovery of the antibiotic streptomycin by Russian biochemist and microbiologist Selman Abraham Waksman, that an effective treatment became possible. However, in the 1980s, drug-resistant strains of tuberculosis began to emerge.

Sadly, for D.H. Lawrence, these discoveries came too late, and he died in Vence in France's Maritime Alps, on 2 March 1930 at the age of forty-four. Frieda died on 11 August 1956. As for Louisa Burrows, in April 1941 she married Frederick Heath, and a year later retired from teaching. She died in 1962, ironically, whilst on holiday in Bournemouth.

J.R.R. Tolkien

In the latter part of his life, philologist and writer John Ronald Reuel Tolkien moved to Bournemouth from Oxford with his wife, Edith, where, away from the hurly-burly of his former home city, he could write in peace. His family originated from Germany, and were makers of the 'Tolkien' upright pianoforte.

John's father Arthur fell on hard times and in 1890, he had travelled from his home in the Midlands of England to South Africa to seek his fortune. There, he became manager of the Bank of Africa at Bloemfontein, capital of the Orange Free State. On 16 April 1891, Arthur married Mabel Suffield, also from the English Midlands, in Cape Town Cathedral, and the couple set up home together in Bloemfontein, where their two sons were born: John Ronald Reuel Tolkien on 3 January 1892, and Hilary Arthur Reuel Tolkien two years later.

In Bloemfontein, John began to suffer from recurrent fevers, so in April 1895, his mother Mabel took him and his brother Hilary back to England to stay with her parents in Birmingham, in order for him to escape the heat. The boys would not see their father again, for Arthur died, following an attack of rheumatic fever, in February 1896.

In the summer of 1896, Mabel and her sons moved into a cottage near Moseley, just to the south of Birmingham. In September 1900, John sat and passed the entrance examination for Birmingham's King Edward VI Grammar School – his late father's school. This meant that Mabel was forced to relocate once more, this time to Hagley Road, Edgbaston.

When, in 1900, Mabel converted to Roman Catholicism, she transferred her sons to a Catholic Grammar School, St Phillip's. Here, she met Francis Morgan, one of the Oratory Fathers (a society of priests) who ran the school. However, Mabel was disappointed with St Phillip's, so she decided to teach John herself, and prepare him (successfully) for a Foundation Scholarship to his former school, King Edward's, to which he returned in the autumn of 1903. Having already lost their father, the Tolkien brothers were now to lose their mother, who was diagnosed with diabetes mellitus in April 1904, for which there was then no treatment. Mabel died in a diabetic coma the following November, at the age of thirty-four.

Father Francis took the boys under his wing and found them lodgings with their widowed maternal aunt, Beatrice Suffield, in Edgbaston. They were not happy here, so early in 1908, he arranged for them to lodge with a Mrs Faulkner, wife of a wine merchant in Duchess Road. This is where Tolkien met and fell in love with Edith Bratt, daughter of a shoemaker from Handsworth, a suburb of Birmingham, who was also one of Mrs Faulkner's lodgers.

In the autumn of 1911, Tolkien, who had been awarded an Open Exhibition in Classics to Exeter College, Oxford, commenced as an undergraduate at the university. Here, in

J.R.R. Tolkien at the Hotel Miramar. (Hotel Miramar)

June 1915, he obtained a First Class honours degree in English Language and Literature. On 22 March 1916, he and Edith were married at the Catholic Church of St Mary Immaculate, Warwick. She would bear him four children. Three months later, as an officer in the Lancashire Fusiliers, he embarked for the Western Front. However, that November, he was invalided out of the Army with trench fever.

After the war, the Tolkiens settled in Oxford, where Tolkien worked on the Oxford English Dictionary as assistant lexicographer. He also gave tutorials in Anglo-Saxon to the undergraduates of St Hugh's College. In 1921 the Tolkiens moved to Leeds, where Tolkien was appointed to the university's English Department. Three years later he became Professor of English Language.

When in September 1925 his five-year-old son Michael, lost his toy dog on the beach whilst the family were on holiday at Filey in Yorkshire, Tolkien wrote *Roverandum*, in order to console him. It is a short story about a dog, Rover, who is magically transformed into a toy.[1] This fantasy story (which was not published until 1997) was a foretaste of things to come. In 1925, the Tolkiens returned to Oxford, where Tolkien took up the post of Professor of Anglo-Saxon at the university.

Tolkien's book *The Hobbit* (published in 1937) reflected his fascination with language, folklore and saga. In it, hairy little creatures of that name inhabit 'Middle Earth', a fictitious world of long ago, in which gnomes, goblins and dragons, with their own language and mythology, become locked in a battle of good against evil. It was his habit to read chapters of *The Hobbit* to his children, of whom Christopher, his third and youngest son, would sometimes discover discrepancies in the text![2] (The same characters which appeared in *The Hobbit* appeared subsequently in the much larger work, *Lord of the Rings*, published in 1954-55).

In 1945, Tolkien was appointed Merton Professor of English Language and Literature at Oxford University, a post which he held until his retirement in 1959. In 1953, the Tolkiens moved from Oxford to 76 Sandfield Road at nearby Headington.

In 1968, when Tolkien was aged seventy-six and his wife Edith was seventy-nine, the couple decided to move from Headington to Bournemouth. There were several reasons for this. Both were becoming increasingly infirm and finding the house and garden at Headington difficult to manage. Also, Tolkien, by now a famous author, was anxious to avoid the 'almost intolerable stream of fan-mail, gifts, telephone calls, and visitors' which he received. Finally, Edith was already familiar with Bournemouth and liked the town very much.

For some years, Edith, who suffered increasingly from arthritis, had taken her holidays at the Hotel Miramar on Bournemouth's East Cliff, which she thoroughly enjoyed. When Tolkien retired he joined her on these holidays, where he sat on the veranda and smoked 'a large and pungent pipe'.[3] He and Edith also enjoyed the company of Douglas and Minnie Steele, proprietors of the hotel, with whom they became good friends.

Although, in Bournemouth, Tolkien missed his Oxford acquaintances, in particular his academic friends with whom he could converse easily on matters of mutual interest. He was gratified to observe that Edith's spirits were better when she was on holiday than when she was at home. The outcome was that the Tolkiens' visits to Bournemouth became increasingly frequent.

On 16 October 1963, Tolkien wrote from the Hotel Miramar to his grandson Michael George Tolkien, to say that he had 'had three rather exhausting experiences since Monday'. The first was when he visited an 'admirer' who lived 'practically next door to this hotel [but who] proved to be stone-deaf, though highly intelligent and well-read'. The second was when 'in the middle of lunch I had to rescue an old lady who was choking on a whiting bone, and get her to a doctor', and the third was when he had to 'entertain another deaf old lady'.[4] In another letter to Michael, written on 1 November 1963, he makes mention of 'the excellent Doctor Tolhurst', who ' …urges me to take no drugs or assistants – except those occasionally prescribed by a doctor: sc. [namely] when a special infection lodges in the weak areas liable to assault'.[5] Dr Denis Tolhurst was the doctor who attended the Tolkiens when they were in Bournemouth, and who, with his wife Jocelyn, also became friends of theirs.

In August 1968, the Tolkiens moved to Bournemouth permanently, but in somewhat traumatic circumstances, as will shortly be seen. Their new home was a three-bedroom bungalow – 'Woodridings', 19 Lakeside Road – which was within a few hundred yards of the beach at Branksome Chine.:

Here, they lived in greater luxury than they had ever known… [and yet] despite the wealth generated by Ronald's [Tolkien's] writing, they both retained a great simplicity in the way they lived. Now, for the first time, they enjoyed the comforts of central heating and a bathroom each; while Edith was as excited as a young bride at the sophistication of their new kitchen! … the garage was converted into a study and office where Joy Hill, who worked for [publisher] Allen & Unwin, would often come to help him with his correspondence, as his popularity spread and letters poured in from fans all over the world, but especially reflecting his extraordinary cult status in the USA.[6]

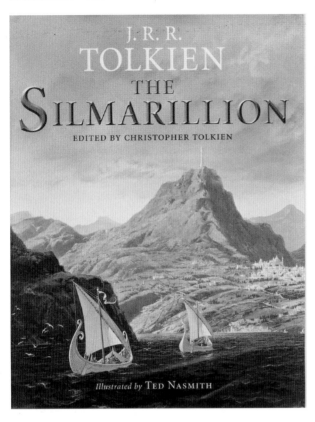

The Silmarillion.

To his son Christopher, on 2 January 1969, Tolkien wrote, 'My library is now in order; and nearly all the things that I thought were lost have turned up'. The fact that he was now living on the south coast had deliberately been kept a secret, in order that he might be enabled to work in peace, and he now devoted himself to *The Silmarillion*, which he had begun in Oxford and which again features 'Middle Earth'. This originally consisted of five separate works, but it was Tolkien's wish that they be published together.

On 20 May 1969, Tolkien wrote a letter to Camilla, daughter of Rayner Unwin of publishers Allen & Unwin, asking the question, 'Is there a God, a Creator-Designer, a Mind to which our minds are akin (being derived from it) so that It is intelligible to us in part'. As a devout Catholic, he evidently decided that there was, for he goes on to declare '…that the chief purpose of life, for any of us, is to increase, according to our capacity, our knowledge of God by all the means we have, and to be moved by it to praise and thanks'.[7]

In that year, 1969, the Tolkien Society was founded by author Vera Chapman, with Tolkien himself as president. There are now similar societies throughout the world.

In May 1971 the Tolkiens, on Dr Tolhurst's advice, took a short holiday in Sidmouth, Devon. In November, Edith, now eighty-two, was taken ill with inflammation of the gall bladder. She died in a Bournemouth nursing home on 29th of that month. Whereupon, Tolkien returned to Oxford, to Merton College, where he had been a Fellow from 1945 to 1959, and where the college now offered him accommodation in a flat at 21 Merton Street. In 1972, Tolkien was awarded the CBE by the Queen, and an Honorary Doctorate of Letters from Oxford University.

On 28 August 1973, Tolkien visited Bournemouth to stay at 22 Little Forest Road, with his friends Dr and Mrs Tolhurst. On Wednesday 29th, he wrote from there to his daughter Priscilla, to say that Mr Causier, the driver of the hire car which had driven him down from Oxford, had '… dropped me off on the East Overcliff by the [Hotel] Miramar, which nostalgically attracted me; but I went into the town & did some shopping, including having a hair trim. I then walked back to the Miramar…'

Woodridings.
(Stephen Malton)

There then followed a series of mishaps. Tolkien lost his bank card and some money, whereupon he attempted to book in at the Hotel Miramar, but was told they had no room available until the following Tuesday. Meanwhile, Causier found him, 'v.g. [very good] rooms for 2 nights'.[8] Tolkien then decided that he would remain in Bournemouth until 11 September. In the event, he died there on 2 September, aged eighty-one. He is buried beside his wife in Wolvercote Cemetery, Oxford.

After Tolkien's death it fell to his son, Christopher (lecturer and tutor in English Language at New College, Oxford from 1964 to 1975), to edit *The Silmarillion* – which his late father had been revising but had failed to complete. It was published in 1977 by Allen & Unwin. On 10 June 1992, Tolkien's daughter Priscilla, arrived at the Hotel Miramar to unveil a plaque in memory of her late father.

When, one fine sunny day – 10 July 2008 – Stephen Malton, proprietor of the Bournemouth-based company Prodem Demolition, set out for work, he was, 'led into an adventure… [which] I could never have dreamt possible'.

Stephen's task was to demolish a bungalow, situated not far from the sea at Branksome Chine, Poole. He had searched the internet, and discovered that the property had once belonged to J.R.R. Tolkien (since when there had been only one other owner). This was of particular interest to Stephen, who, as a small boy, had enjoyed the adventures of Bilbo Baggins (the protagonist of *The Hobbit*, and only six months previously, had painted a large portrait of Tolkien's fictional character 'Gollum').

Stephen describes what happened when he passed through the side gate of 19 Lakeside Road:

Walking through the overgrown garden… my foot got caught on what I thought at the time was a large rock. Slowly parting the grass with my hands, I suddenly found myself face to face with a lion. The hypnotic look of stone eyes stared back at me.

There were, in fact, two stone lions; the discovery of which led Stephen to conduct a thorough search. The outcome was, that further 'treasures' revealed themselves, 'not only in the garden but also in the house, that had lain hidden for some forty years'.

For Stephen, the moment of greatest excitement came when he removed the fireplace and discovered three postcards which had fallen down behind it. On one was depicted an image of T.E. Lawrence; on the second, the painting 'Midsummer' by Albert Moore. Both of these were unwritten. The third, however, bore an Irish postage stamp, dated (19)68, an image of an Irish landscape, and the following handwritten text (several words of which are illegible):

> July 19
> I have been thinking of you a lot and hoping everything has gone as well as could be expected in the most difficult circumstances. We have had a few good walks and lots of drives - - various peninsulas and agree that the seascapes are really lovely – as are the hedgerows. Our love to Ronald. We hope he is - - - to - .
> Lin

The postcard had been sent the month before the Tolkiens had moved permanently to Bournemouth. The sender, 'Lin', is believed to be the American writer Linwood Vrooman Carter, author of works of science fiction and fantasy, who usually abbreviated his name in this way. (Carter wrote *Tolkien: A Look behind 'The Lord of the Rings'*, a study of the works of Tolkien, which was published in 1969, the year after he sent the postcard).

The 'difficult circumstances' to which Carter referred on his postcard is a reference to the fact that, on 17 June 1968, Tolkien was hurrying down the stairs of his Oxford home, when he fell heavily and had to be admitted to the nearby Nuffield Orthopaedic Centre. In his words:

> I…never went back again – never saw my room, or my house [in Oxford], again. In addition to the shock of the fall and the operation, this has had a queer effect. It is like reading a story and coming to a sudden break…For a long time I felt that I was in a (bad) dream…[9]

Stephen Malton in the late J.R.R. Tolkien's garden, with one of the Tolkien 'treasures' that he discovered.

The fireplace from Woodridings with Stephen Malton's depiction of Tolkien's fictional character 'Gollum', which he painted prior to making his great discovery! (Stephen Malton)

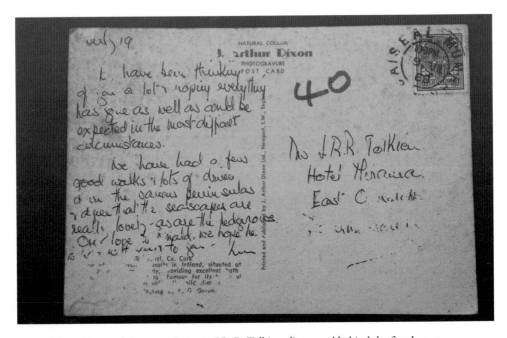

Postcard from Linwood Vrooman Carter to J.R.R. Tolkien, discovered behind the fireplace at Woodridings. (Stephen Malton)

Appendix

The family tree of Gervis, Tapps, and Meyrick

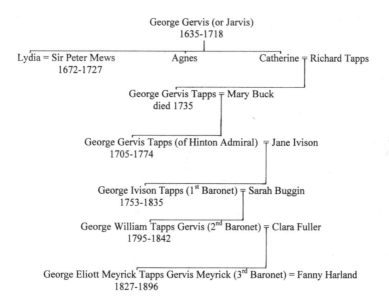

George Gervis (or Jarvis)
1635-1718

Lydia = Sir Peter Mews   Agnes   Catherine ⊤ Richard Tapps
1672-1727

George Gervis Tapps ⊤ Mary Buck
died 1735

George Gervis Tapps (of Hinton Admiral) ⊤ Jane Ivison
1705-1774

George Ivison Tapps (1st Baronet) ⊤ Sarah Buggin
1753-1835

George William Tapps Gervis (2nd Baronet) ⊤ Clara Fuller
1795-1842

George Eliott Meyrick Tapps Gervis Meyrick (3rd Baronet) = Fanny Harland
1827-1896

The family tree of Smith

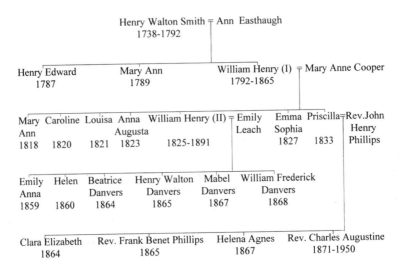

Henry Walton Smith ⊤ Ann Easthaugh
1738-1792

Henry Edward
1787

Mary Ann
1789

William Henry (I) ⊤ Mary Anne Cooper
1792-1865

Mary Ann 1818   Caroline 1820   Louisa 1821   Anna Augusta 1823   William Henry (II) 1825-1891 ⊤ Emily Leach   Emma Sophia 1827   Priscilla 1833 ⊤ Rev.John Henry Phillips

Emily Anna 1859   Helen 1860   Beatrice Danvers 1864   Henry Walton Danvers 1865   Mabel Danvers 1867   William Frederick Danvers 1868

Clara Elizabeth 1864   Rev. Frank Benet Phillips 1865   Helena Agnes 1867   Rev. Charles Augustine 1871-1950

The family tree of Tregonwell

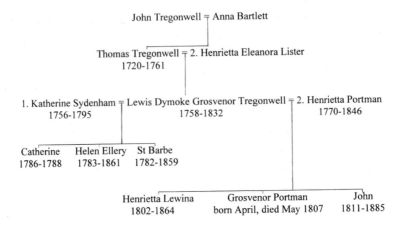

John Tregonwell ⊤ Anna Bartlett

Thomas Tregonwell ⊤ 2. Henrietta Eleanora Lister
1720-1761

1. Katherine Sydenham 1756-1795 ⊤ Lewis Dymoke Grosvenor Tregonwell 1758-1832 ⊤ 2. Henrietta Portman 1770-1846

Catherine 1786-1788   Helen Ellery 1783-1861   St Barbe 1782-1859

Henrietta Lewina 1802-1864   Grosvenor Portman born April, died May 1807   John 1811-1885

Epilogue

This has been the story of how Bournemouth – formerly the home of rabbits and small reptiles, birds and deer – became the bustling town that it is today, and all in the space of two centuries. Many noteworthy personalities played their part in this transformation, and there are many more who might have easily found their way into the pages of this book – including politicians, businessmen and women, smugglers and spies, and even murderers! However, a choice had to be made, and in the event, those chosen were selected either for their exceptional gifts, learning or altruism, or because they played a pivotal role in the evolution of the town.

> I mind so much about the future: what we are going to leave for our children and grandchildren. That is what really gets me.[1]

How well these words – spoken by HM The Prince of Wales in 2008, the year in which he celebrated his sixtieth birthday – resonate with the sentiments of Tregonwell, Gervis, Ferrey, Burton, Lacey and others who played their part in the creation of the beautiful town of Bournemouth. (This, of course, is not to say that some of the former did not have an additional pecuniary interest in their endeavours!)

This book commenced with a discussion of how the first pine trees came to be planted in Bournemouth; thus bestowing on the town an aesthetic beauty which was, and continues to be, admired by all. Pine trees are synonymous with Bournemouth and it is no coincidence that the pine cone appears atop Bournemouth's coat-of-arms. And just as each great pine tree grows from a small cone, so the great town of Bournemouth grew from equally small beginnings.

When Stephen Malton set out for work that July day in 2008, he could never have imagined that he would discover a collection of artefacts – 'treasures' – which had once belonged to his favourite boyhood author and former Bournmeouth resident, J.R.R. Tolkien. Surely, further facts about the town's remarkable history remain to be discovered!

NOTES

INTRODUCTION

1.   Poulet, Lord Thomas. 1574. Calendar of Domestic State Papers.
2.   Young, David S. *The Story of Bournemouth*, p.20.
3.   *Ibid*, p.30.

ONE

1.   Mate, C.H. and Charles Riddle. *Bournemouth 1810-1910*, p.35.
2.   Information supplied by Sir George Meyrick, 7th Baronet.
3.   Document of Sale for land purchased by L.D.G Tregonwell from Sir George Ivison Tapps, dated 25 September 1810.
4.   Malmesbury Tithe Survey, 1796, Volume 2, p.15 (MS).
5.   Document compiled by Sir George Tapps in 1790, prior to various sales of land and property made by him to Sir George Rose, HCRO 2M30/348.

TWO

1.   Sydenham, Dr G.F. *The History of the Sydenham Family*, p.550.
2.   *Ibid*, pp.552-54.
3.   Information kindly supplied by Mrs Julia E. Smith, and by The Keep Military Museum, Dorchester.
4.   Malmesbury Tythe Survey, 1796, Volume 2, p.15.
5.   Mate, C.H. and Charles Riddle. *Bournemouth 1810-1910*, p.57.
6.   Young, David S. *The Story of Bournemouth*, p.45.
7.   Graham, Mary. *The Royal National Hospital: The Story of Bournemouth's Sanatorium*, p.19.

FOUR

1.   Granville, Augustus Bozzi. *The Spas of England: Southern Spas*, p.527.
2.   Post Office Directory for Hampshire, 1859. London: Kelly & Co.
3.   Sydenham, John (Publisher). *The Visitor's Guide to Bournemouth and its Neighbourhood*. (1840).

FIVE

1.   Mate, C.H. and Charles Riddle. *Bournemouth 1810-1910*, p.90.

SIX

1.   Bournemouth estate: Reports of Mr Decimus Burton 1845-1856. London: Crawley Arnold.

SEVEN

1.   Granville, Augustus Bozzi. *The Spas of England: Southern Spas*, p.513.
2.   *Ibid*, pp.514,516.
3.   *Ibid*, p.512.
4.   *Ibid*, pp.520,523-24,533.

5.   *Ibid*, p.526.
6.   Mate, C.H. and Charles Riddle. *Bournemouth 1810-1910*, pp.83-4.

EIGHT

1.   'Bournemouth in the Good Old Days: The Rev. A.S. Bennett Reminisces'. 27 October 1904. The *Bournemouth Graphic*.
2.   McQueen, Ian. The East Parley Mission, written for the centenary of St Barnabas' Chapel in 1963.
3.   Young, David S. *The Story of Bournemouth*, p.113.
4.   *Ibid*, p.115.

NINE

1.   Talbot, Mary Anne. *The History of Talbot Village*, p.10.
2.   *Ibid*, pp.10-11.
3.   *Ibid*, p.7.
4.   *Ibid*, p.6.
5.   *Ibid*, pp.4,5.
6.   *Ibid*, pp.7-8.
7.   *Ibid*, p.9.
8.   *Ibid*, p.4.
9.   *Bournemouth Times and Directory*, 6 March 1935.

TEN

1.   Young, David S. *The Story of Bournemouth*, p.207.
2.   Samuel, Olive J. *Boscombe Manor*, p.25.

ELEVEN

1.   Mate, C.H. and Charles Riddle. *Bournemouth 1810-1910*, pp.109,110,117.
2.   *Bournemouth Times*, 21 May 1934.
3.   Mate, *op.cit.*, p.121.
4.   *Ibid*, p.165.
5.   Bournemouth Visitors Directory, 26 May 1886.

TELVE

1.   Sanatorium for Consumption, Bournemouth. (Report) 1854 by Charles Pannel. Extracted from Brompton Hospital Annual Report 1854.
2.   Mate, C.H. and Charles Riddle. *Bournemouth 1810-1910*, p.232.
3.   Royal National Sanatorium, 1855-1955.
4.   The Forty-Fourth Annual Report of the National Sanatorium (1898)
5.   Graham, Mary. *The Royal National Hospital: The Story of Bournemouth's Sanatorium*, p.43.

THIRTEEN

1.   Hambleden Papers N/6, n.d.
2.   Chilston, Viscount. *WH Smith*, p.14.
3.   Hambleden Papers HA/8/2, 28 September 1860.

4. Chilston, *op.cit.*, p.43.
5. Holy Bible, New Testament Book of John, 13:3 and 11:25.
6. The Forty-Third Annual Report of the National Sanatorium (1898).
7. Graham, Mary. *The Royal National Hospital: The Story of Bournemouth's Sanatorium*, p.67.
8. Bussby, Canon Frederick. *Holy Trinity Church*, p.30.
9. University of Birmingham Information Services, Special Collections Department, Main Library, Edgbaston Campus. DA21/1/2/36.

FOURTEEN
1. Graham, Mary. *The Royal National Hospital: The Story of Bournemouth's Sanatorium*, p.6.
2. *Ibid*, p.8.
3. Mate, C.H. and Charles Riddle. *Bournemouth 1810-1910*, p.231.
4. Graham, *op.cit.*, p.35.
5. *Ibid*. 'Dietary Table'.
6. *Ibid*, p.57.

SEVENTEEN
1. Herkomer, Hubert von. *Autobiography*, privately printed. 1890.
2. Bazaar. 1 May 1896.

EIGTEEN
1. Hampshire Record Office. 123A03/A2/5(1).
2. *Ibid*. 123A03/A2/8.
3. *Ibid*. 123A03/A2/9.

TWENTY
1. Russell-Cotes, Sir Merton. *Home and Abroad*. p.21.
2. Information kindly provided by the Royal Bath Hotel, from article written by Phebe Lankester – under the nom de plume 'Penelope' – for *The Queen* magazine.
3. Sydenham, John (Publisher). *The Visitor's Guide to Bournemouth and its Neighbourhood*, p.11.
4. *Ibid*, p.4.
5. *Ibid*, p.11.

TWENTY-ONE
1. Langtry, Lillie. *Lillie Langtry*, p.13.
2. *Ibid*, p.187.
3. *Ibid*, p.29.
4. *Ibid*, p.77.
5. Hillsdon, Sonia. *The Jersey Lily*, p.45.
6. Langtry, *op.cit.*, p.103.
7. *Ibid*, p.196.
8. *Ibid*, p.179.
9. Hillsdon, *op.cit.*, p.126.
10. Information kindly supplied by Anthony Le Gallais.

11.   Beatty, Laura, *Lillie Langtry*, pp.131–32.
12.   *Ibid*, pp.177,187.
13.   *Ibid*, p.198.
14.   Information kindly supplied by Anthony Le Gallais.

TWENTY-TWO
1.   Dobell, Horace, MD. *The Medical Aspects of Bournemouth and its Surroundings*, pp.14-15,18.
2.   *Ibid*, p.9.
3.   *Ibid*, pp.16, 17.
4.   *Ibid*, p.19.
5.   *Ibid*, p.23.
6.   *Ibid*, pp.6,7.
7.   *Ibid*, p.3.
8.   *Ibid*, p.165.
9.   *Ibid*, p.166.
10.   Kinsey-Morgan, *Bournemouth as a Health Resort*, p.85.
11.   *Ibid*, p.88.
12.   Chemists and Druggist's Diary, 1888.
13.   Kinsey-Morgan, op.cit., p.90.
14.   *Ibid*, p.91.
15.   *Ibid*, pp.164–65.
16.   *Ibid*, p.20.

TWENTY-THREE
1.   Mate, C.H. and Charles Riddle. *Bournemouth 1810-1910*, p.264.
2.   Taylor, Una. *Guests and Memories*, p.360.
3.   *Ibid*, p.264.
4.   *Ibid*, p.364.

TWENTY-FOUR
1.   The *Bournemouth Graphic*. 14 April 1910.
2.   County Borough of Bournemouth. Report of Deputation appointed to visit various Towns for the purpose of inspecting Town Halls and Municipal Offices, Etc. 23 March – 2 April 1900. Bournemouth: Bright's Ltd.
3.   'Bournemouth in the Good Old Days: The Rev. A.S. Bennett Reminisces'. 27 October 1904. The *Bournemouth Graphic*.
4.   Bournemouth Municipal Buildings. Law Courts & Town Hall. Report, 17 February 1906. Bournemouth: Holland Rowbottom.

TWENTY-FIVE
1.   Churchill, Winston S. *My Early Life*, pp.37-38.

TWENTY-SIX
1.   *Bournemouth Echo*, 12 December 1991.
2.   Letter from Percy I Newlyn to the *Bournemouth Daily Echo*, published 27 April 1914.

3.   Newlyn, Percy I, *Bournemouth Daily Echo*, 27 April 1940.
4.   Crawley, Lieutenant Colonel Chetwode. 1931. *From Telegraphy to Television*, p.83.
5.   Woodland, W. Lloyd. 1952. Assize Pageant: Fifty Years in the Criminal Court. Harrap, p.14.

TWENTY-SEVEN

1.   Lindsay, Gillian. *Flora Thompson*, p.70.
2.   Lane, Margaret. 1957. Essay on Flora Thompson. The Cornhill, No. 1011.
3.   Flora Thompson. 9 May 1914. His Lady of the Lilacs. *The Ladies Companion*.
4.   Thompson, Flora. *Heatherley*, Chapter 3. Published 1979 in A Country Calendar, edited by Margaret Lane. Oxford: Oxford University Press.

TWENTY-EIGHT

1.   Boulton, James T. (editor.) *Lawrence in Love*, p.xii.
2.   *Ibid*, p.150.
3.   *Ibid*, p.151.
4.   *Ibid*, p.152.
5.   *Ibid*, p.153.
6.   Huxley, Aldous (editor.) *The Letters of DH Lawrence*, p.16.
7.   *Ibid*, p.17.
8.   *Ibid*, pp.18,19.
9.   *Ibid*, pp.158-59.
10.   Edwards, Elizabeth. *Bournemouth Past*, p.114.
11.   Huxley, op.cit., p.22.
12.   *Ibid*, p.165.
13.   *Ibid*, p.165.
14.   Lawrence, DH. *Sons and Lovers*, pp. 221,224-25.
15.   *Ibid*, p.362.
16.   *Ibid*, p.222.

TWENTY-NINE

1.   Tolkien, John and Priscilla. *The Tolkien Family Album*, p.49.
2.   *Ibid*, p.58.
3.   *Ibid*, p.55.
4.   Carpenter, Humphrey (editor.) *Letters of J.R.R. Tolkien*, p.336.
5.   *Ibid*, p.340.
6.   Tolkien, op.cit., pp.83-4.
7.   Carpenter, op.cit., p.400.
8.   *Ibid*, p.531.
9.   *Ibid*, p.395.

EPILOGUE

1.   *Charles at 60: the Passionate Prince*. BBC television documentary, 12 November 2008.

Bibliography

Anderson, Roy C. 1995. *Bournemouth and Poole Tramways*. Midhurst, West Sussex: Middleton Press.

Beatty, Laura. 2000. *Lillie Langtry*. London: Random House.

Blachford, John. *St Peter's, Bournemouth*. Bournemouth: Grafica.

Boulton, James T. (ed.) 1968. *Lawrence in Love*. Nottingham: University of Nottingham.

Bournemouth, Christchurch and Poole Directory for 1874-75. London: Butcher, Cole & Co.

Bournemouth estate: Reports of Mr Decimus Burton 1845-1856. London: Crawley Arnold.

Bournemouth. Municipal Buildings. Law Courts & Town Hall. Report, 17 February 1906. Bournemouth, Holland Rowbottom.

Bournemouth Times and Directory, 6 March 1935.

Bournemouth Visitors Directory, 3 April 1886. Death of Sir Henry Taylor KCB.

Bussby, Canon Frederick. 1969. *Holy Trinity Church*. Wimborne, Dorset: WE Collins.

Carpenter, Humphrey (editor.) 1981. *Letters of J.R.R. Tolkien*. London: George Allen & Unwin.

Chilston, Viscount. 1965. *WH Smith*. London: Routledge & Kegan Paul.

Churchill, Winston S. 1972. *My Early Life*. London: Collins.

Civilian, The. 14 May 1921.

Coleridge, Sir J.T. 1870. *A Memoir of the Rev. John Keble, M.A.* Oxford and London: James Parker & Co.

County Borough of Bournemouth. Report of Deputation appointed to visit various Towns for the purpose of inspecting Town Halls and Municipal Offices, Etc. 23 March – 2 April 1900. Bournemouth: Bright's Ltd.

Daily Echo, Bournemouth.

Dobell, Horace, MD. 1886. *The Medical Aspects of Bournemouth and its Surroundings*. London: Smith, Elder.

Dobell, Mrs Horace. 1910. *The Poetical Works of Mrs Horace Dobell*. London: Smith, Elder.

Edwards, Elizabeth. 1998. *Bournemouth Past*. Chichester, UK: Phillimore.

Gittings, Robert. 1978. *Young Thomas Hardy*. London: Penguin Books.

Goss, Edmund. and Robert Louis Stevenson. *Encyclopaedia Britannica*, 11th Edition.

Graham, Mary. 1992. *The Royal National Hospital: The Story of Bournemouth's Sanatorium*. Bournemouth Local Studies Publications.

Granville, Augustus Bozzi. 1841. *The Spas of England: Southern Spas*. London: Henry Colburn.

Hardy, Florence Emily. 1962. *The Life of Thomas Hardy*. London: Macmillan & Co.

Hillsdon, Sonia. 1996. *The Jersey Lily*. Bradford on Avon, Wiltshire: Seaflower Books.

Huxley, Aldous (editor.) 1932. *The Letters of DH Lawrence*. London: William Heinemann.

Kinsey-Morgan A. 1889. *Bournemouth as a Health Resort*. London: Simpkin Marshall and Co.

Langtry Lillie. 1989. *The Days I Knew*. St John, Jersey, Channel Islands: Redberry Press.

Lawrence, D.H. 1994. *Sons and Lovers*. London: Compact Books.

Letters of Robert Louis Stevenson, The, Volume I, Project Gutenberg (undated.)

Lindsay, Gillian. 2007. *Flora Thompson*. London: Robert Hale.

Mate, C.H. and Charles Riddle. 1910. *Bournemouth 1810-1910*. Bournemouth: Messrs. W. Mate & Sons.

Medlicott, C.L. and W.A. Camp. 1996. *St Mark's Church, Talbot Village: A Victorian Dream*.

Messum, David. 1976. *The Life and Work of Lucy Kemp-Welch*. Antique Collectors Club.

Parker, Eric. 1924. *Hesketh Prichard*. London: T. Fisher Unwin.

Ransom, W.P. 1991. *Bournemouth Trams and Trolleybuses*. Bournemouth Local Studies Publications.

Russell-Cotes, Sir Merton. 1921. *Home and Abroad*. Bournemouth: Richmond Hill Printing Works.

Sakula, Alex. 1983. Augustus Bozzi Granville. *Journal of the Royal Society of Medicine*, October 1983, Volume 76-10, pp.876-82.

Samuel, Olive J. 2004. *Boscombe Manor*. Christchurch: Natula Publications.

St Peter's, Bournemouth. 2006. Norwich: Jarrold Publishing.

Sydenham, Dr G.F. 1928. *The History of the Sydenham Family*. East Molesey, Surrey: E. Dwelly (privately printed.)

Sydenham, John (Publisher). 1840. *The Visitor's Guide to Bournemouth and its Neighbourhood*.

Talbot, Mary Anne. 1873. *The History of Talbot Village*. Piccadilly: Hatchards Publishers.

Taylor, Una. 1924. *Guests and Memories*. London: Humphrey Milford, Oxford University Press.

Thompson, Captain C.W. (compiler.) 1894. *Records of the Dorset Yeomanry*. Dorchester: Dorset County Chronicle Printing Works.

Tolkien, John and Priscilla. 1992. *The Tolkien Family Album*. London: HarperCollins.

Tregonwell estate Account Book 1846-1884.

Walker, John. 2007. *The Story of Bournemouth*.

Walker, John. 2004. *St Peter's Church, Bournemouth: Notable Personal Memorials in the Church and Churchyard*.

Wilson, Charles. 1985. *First with the News*. London: Jonathan Cape.

Woodhead, Felicity A. 1994. *Flora of the Christchurch Area*. Shaftesbury: Blackmore Press.

Young, David S. 1957. *The Story of Bournemouth*. London: Robert Hale.

Index

Aitken, Dr, 37

Alum Bay, 124,155

Alum Chine, 15,69,88,92,110,119-21

Anderson, 14,16,17,20

Aragon, Catherine of, 14

Arbuthnot, Harriet, 20

Argyll, Duke of, 87

Auvergne, 102-04

Bath Hotel, see Royal Bath Hotel

Bathe, Sir Hugo de, 97

Bathe, Lady de – see Lillie Langtry

Battenburg, Henry of, 89

Battenburg, Prince Louis, 96

Baxter, Charles, 108,109

Beale, Alderman J.E., 119

Beatrice, Princess, 89

Belle Vue Hotel, 38,52,92

Bennett, Revd Alexander Morden,
   5,38-43,49,69,70,73,82

Bennett, Revd Alexander Sykes, 38-40,43

Bennett, Elizabeth Ann, 39

Bennett, Maria Sarah (née Pike), 39

Bennett, Marianne Elizabeth, 39

Bernhardt, Sarah, 96

Black Beauty, 76,77,80

Bloxworth, 14

Bodley Scott, Dr Thomas, 112,113

Boscombe Manor, 47,50,70,90,110,114

Boscombe Pier, 49,92

Boudant, Professor M., 104

Bournemouth as a Health Resort, 10,88,104

Bournemouth College of Art, 50,78

Bournemouth Commissioners, 53,55,88

Bournemouth Daily Echo, 122,125

Bournemouth Graphic, The, 38,126

Bournemouth Library, 125,130

Bournemouth Pier, 26,34,51,53,84,87,88,92,118,
   124,125

Bournemouth Sanitary Hospital, 103

Bournemouth Tramway, 116,118

Bozzi, Carlo, 35

Branksome Tower, 49,55,57,118

Branksome Dene, 69,121,122

Braun, Karl Ferdinand, 126

Brehmer, Dr Hermann, 56

Brompton Hospital, London,
   56,57,59,65,66,69,70,71

Brookside, 83

Browne, Dr Harold, 43

Browne, Dr Isaac Lennox, 104

Brownsea Island, 19,58

Buller, Mr Justice, 16

Burrows, Louisa, 133, 135,136

Burslem, Dr Willoughby Marshall, 69,70

Burton, Decimus, 11,31,32-4,115

Bussby, Canon Frederick, 67

Byron, Lord George Gordon, 47,72

Carter, Linwood Vrooman, 142,144

Chatto & Windus, 109

Christchurch, 9-13,16,19,23,26,38,39,49,51,55,
   70,71,76,88,118,120,130,135

Christchurch Hospital, 71

Churchill, Lady, 121
Churchill, Lord Randolph, 121
Churchill, Winston Leonard Spencer, 78,121
Clapcott, William, 10
Clark, Emmy, 86
Clark, John King, 86
Clerke, Benjamin, 12
Clerke, Joseph Jarvis, 12
Clutterbuck, Revd B.R., 46
Colvin, Sir Sidney, 108-110
County Gates, 116
Cranborne Lodge, 16,20,45,50-
    3,55,57,70,87,115
Creeke, Christopher Crabbe,
    45,50-3,55,57,70,87,115
Creeke, Elizabeth (née Norwood), 51

Darwin, Charles Robert, 74,75
Darwin, Emma, 74
Davos, Switzerland, 107,112
Dean, William, 10
Dickens, Charles, 69
Dobell, Elizabeth Mary (née Fordham),
    100,102
Dobell, Dr Horace Benge, 100-05,113
Dobell, Sydney Thompson, 101
Dorset Volunteer Rangers, 16
Douglas House, 71
Durrant, George, 33,57,69

Edmonsham House, 17
Edward III, King, 88
Edward VII, King, 55,70,87,92,93,95-7,99
Emmanuel III, King Victor, 127
Enclosure Award, 10,11
Exeter House, 11,17,19-22
Exeter, Marchioness of, 19

Falls, Dr William Stewart, 70,100
Ferrey, Ann (née Lucas), 26
Ferrey, Benjamin, 23,26,27,29,30,31,115
Fire Station, 118
Firs Home, 117
Fogerty, John Frederick, 89
Fox, George, 20

Garner, Shaun, 92
Garnett, Edward, 134,135
George IV, King, 16
Gervis, Sir George William Tapps, 11,23,25,26,31
Gervis, Lady, 34,39
Gladstone, W.E., 96
Godfrey, Dan, 70
Godwin, Mary Wollstonecraft, 47
Godwin, William, 47
Gold Maker's Village, The, 45
Gosse, Edmund, 108,109,110,111,114
Granville, Dr Augustus Bozzi, 10,26,33,35,37
Granville, Mrs (née Kerr), 35,37
Guest, Cornelia – see Lady Wimborne

Hahnemann Convalescent Home, 55,58
Hahnemann, Dr Christian Friedrich Samuel, 55
Hambleden, Lord, 66
Hambledon, Viscountess, 66
Hamerton, Philip Gilbert, 108,110
Hardy, Emma Lavinia, 84,85
Hardy, Thomas, 84,85,108,110,113
Haven Hotel, 126
Henry VIII, King, 14
Herbert Hospital, 71
Herkomer, Professor Hubert von, 78
Hertz, Heinrich, 123
Highcliffe Children's Home, 71
Hinton Admiral, 11
Hodson, Henrietta, 96
Holdenhurst, 10,11,12,22,51,55,118
Holy Trinity Church, 22,43 54,67,68,117
Hopkins, Marianne Elizabeth – see Bennett
Howard, Pamela, 99
Humby, Dr W.W., 69
Hunt, James Henry Leigh, 47,49

Iford, 10,13
Ingram, Samuel, 34
Irving, Sir Henry, 49,90,92

Jenkin, Professor and Mrs Fleeming, 107,110,111
Jones, Arthur Clarence, 98,99
Jones, Arthur Heron, 99
Jones, Maria, 99

Keble, Charlotte (née Clarke), 82
Keble, Revd John, 42,82,83
Kelvin, Lord, 125,126
Kemp-Welch, Edith, 76,80,81
Kemp-Welch, Edwin Buckland, 76
Kemp-Welch, Elizabeth (née Oakes), 76
Kemp-Welch, Lucy, 76-9,81
Kemp-Welch, Martin, 81
Kerr, Miss – see Granville
King's Park, 10,119
Kinsey-Morgan, A., 104
Kinson, 10,40
Koch, Robert, 102

Lacey, Frederick William, 115-120
Lainston Villa, 53
Lamb, Edward Buckton, 57,69
Lambton, Lucinda, 92
Langtry, Edward, 93,94,96-8
Langtry, Lillie, 93-7,99
Langtry Manor Hotel, 95,97,99
Lankester, Sir Edwin Ray, 87
Law Courts, 25,115,118
Lawrence, David Herbert, 133-36
Lawrence, Frieda (née von Richthoven), 136
Le Breton, Emilie Charlotte – see Langtry
Le Breton, Jeanne Marie, 96-8
Le Breton, Very Revd William Corbet, 93
Leven and Melville, Earl of, 119,130
Liberty of Westover, 9,11
Linford Sanatorium, 71
Lloyd George, David, 71
Lubbock, John, 74

Macfie, Dr Ronald Campbell, 131,132
Madeira Hotel, 124,125,127
Mainwaring, Dr Edward Vincent, 69
Malcolm, Ian, 97
Malcolm, Mary, 98
Malmesbury, Lord, 10,12
Malton, Stephen, 141,142,144
Mansion, The – see Exeter House
Marconi, Guglielmo, 123-27
Marie Louise, Princess, 80
Mary, Queen, 14

Mate, Charles H., 11
Matlock, George, 70,71
Meadows, Alfred, 103
Mews, Sir Peter, 8,11
Mews, Lady Lydia, 8
Meyrick, Clara – see Tapps
Meyrick, Lady Fanny, (née Harland), 31
Meyrick, Sir George Eliott Meyrick Tapps Gervis,
    31,58,118,119
Meyrick, Lady Jacintha, 119
Meyrick Park, 10,118,119
Milne, Thomas, 12
Milton, Viscount, 16
Mont Dore, Hotel, 55,58,59,71,103-06,117,118
Moordown, 10,22,25,31,39,118,125
Morden College, Blackheath, Kent, 38,82
Morgan, Father Francis, 137
Morton, Dr Richard, 102
Morton, William Scott, 89
Mudeford, 10,16,38,39

Norris, Philip, 10,13,38

Old Shaftesbury Hall, 126
Olding, F.A., 125
Osbourne, Fanny Vandegrift – see Stevenson
Osbourne, Lloyd, 108
Oscar II, King, 103
Oxford Movement, 82

Packe, C.W., 49,55,57
Pannel, Catherine Louisa, 56,61,
Pannel, Charles Lavington, 56-9,61,82
Pavilion, 88,92
Pearce, Edmund, 39
Phillips, Revd Charles Augustine, 66,67
Phillips, Revd John Henry, 66,68
Phillips, Priscilla (née Smith) 66,68
Pigrome, Nurse, 70
Pike, Maria Sarah, see Bennett
Pokesdown, 13,31,39,50,115,118
Poldhu, Cornwall, 126
Poole, 9,10,12,13,16,19,20,25,32,33,37,50,55,58,
    75,76,81,105,116,118,121,126,135,141
Poor Law, 44

Portman Lodge, 17,20-2
Portman, Lord Henry William, 16
Post Office, 117,123,128,132
Preece, William, 123
Prescott, Revd Oldfield K., 70
Prince of Wales, Charles, 147
Prince of Wales – see Edward VII, King
Priory, The, 14-17,20,21
Prospect Mount – see Terrace Mount
Pugin, A.N. Welby, 30
Pugin, Augustus, 26,30
Pumiline, 104,106

Queen's Park, 12,119

Ranelagh, Lord, 98
Rennie, George, 53
Richardson, Richard, 10
Richmond Hill Congregational Church,
   43,53,117
Riddle, Charles, 130
Roost, The, 73
Royal Academy, 35,78,81
Royal Bath Hotel 27-9,36,55,87,92,116,117
Royal Bournemouth Hospital, 58-60,65,71
Royal Exeter Hotel, 22,117
Royal Institute of British Architects, 30,34
Royal National Hospital, 71,148-50
Royal Victoria Hospital, Gloucester Road,
   55,127
Russell-Cotes Art Gallery & Museum,
   81,87,91,92,116
Russell-Cotes, Lady Annie Nelson (née Clark),
   86,87,89,90
Russell-Cotes, Sir Merton,
   55,86,87,89,91,129,139
Rutland, Duke of, 9

Sanatorium, Royal National, 31,56-9,60,61,64-
   7,69,70,71,82,100, 117
Sargent, John Singer, 110,112
Scarlett, Shelley Leopold Lawrence, 50
Sewell, Anna, 76
Shelley, Harriet (née Westbrook), 47,48
Shelley, Ianthe, 47

Shelley, Lady Jane (née Gibson), 48
Shelley, Mary Wollstonecraft (née Godwin), 47
Shelley, Percy Bysshe, 47,49,50
Shelley, Sir Percy Florence, 47-50,70,73
Shelley, Sir Timothy, 47,48
Skerryvore, 110,111,113,114,128
Slade, Darren, 122
Smith, Anna (née Easthaugh), 62
Smith, Anna Augusta, 64
Smith, Emily (née Leach), 64,66
Smith, Emma, 62
Smith, Hon. Frederick Danvers (see Lord
   Hambleden), 66
Smith, Henry Edward, 62
Smith, Henry Walton, 62-4
Smith, Julia E., 15,17,21,24
Smith, Mary Anne (née Cooper), 62
Smith, Dr W. Allis, 100
Smith, William Henry (WH Smith I), 62,64
Smith, William Henry (WH Smith II), 62,64,66
Southbourne, 10,92,118
Spas of England, The, 10,26,35,36,148,153
Springbourne, 12,50,130
St Andrew's Presbyterian Church, 43,117
Steele, Douglas, 139
Steele, Minnie, 139
Stern's Pine Extract, 104
Stevenson, Fanny Vandegrift, 107,109,111-13
Stevenson, Margaret Isabella Balfour, 107
Stevenson, Robert Louis Balfour, 49,73,103,107-
   09,111,113,128
St John, Canon M.W.F., 49
St Mary's Home for Invalid Ladies, 58
St Peter's Church, 24,25,28,38-43,46,48,49-
   51,55,69,
   70,73,83,84,100,102,117,134
Street, George Edmund, 25,40,42,46,57,64
St Stephen's Church, 43,117
Sumner, Bishop Charles Richard, 38,40
Sydenham, Ellery (née Williams), 14
Sydenham, Dr G.F., 14
Sydenham, Helen Ellery, 14
Sydenham, Katherine – see Tregonwell
Sydenham, St Barbe (senior), 14-16,17
Sydenham, St Barbe (junior), 14,16,20

Sykes, Dr Walter J., 104

Symes Cottage – see Portman Lodge

Talbot, Sir George, 44

Talbot, Georgina Charlotte, 45,46,128

Talbot, Mary Anne, 44,45,128

Talbot Village, 44-6,128

Tapps Arms – see Tregonwell Arms

Tapps, Lady Clara, 23

Tapps, George Gervis, 11,12,53,69

Tapps, Sir George Ivison, 11,13,23

Tapps, George William, 13,23,25

Taylor, George, 72

Taylor, Sir Henry, 70,72,73,110,112,113

Taylor, John Henry, 119

Taylor, Lady Theodosia Alicia Ellen Charlotte (née Sping Rice), 72,73,110,112,114

Taylors of Loughborough, 42

Terrace Mount, 17,19

Terry, Ellen, 49

Thomas, John, 88,90,91,92

Thompson, Edwin, 128,132

Thompson, Flora Jane (née Timms), 128,129,131

Thompson, Henry Basil,

Thompson, John, 128

Thompson, Peter Redmond, 132

Thompson, Sydney, 101

Thompson, Winifred Grace, 129

Throop, 10

Times, The, 56,57,71,103

Titanic, RMS, 126,131

Tolhurst, Dr and Mrs Denis, 139,140

Tolkien, Christopher, 138,140,141

Tolkien, Hilary Arthur Reuel, 137

Tolkien, John Ronald Reuel, 137-44,147

Tolkien, Mabel (née Suffield), 137

Tolkien, Michael George, 139

Town Hall, 31,49,53-5,106,118

Tregonwell Arms, 13,17,20

Tregonwell Estate Account Book 1846-1884, 20

Tregonwell, Grosvenor Portman, 14

Tregonwell, Henrietta (née Portman), 16,17,19,20,21

Tregonwell, Henrietta Lewina, 16

Tregonwell, Sir John, 14

Tregonwell, John, 22,23

Tregonwell, Katherine (née Sydneham), 14-16

Tregonwell, Lewis Dymoke Grosvenor, 10,13-17,19-23,33,37

Trelawney, Edward John, 47

Trim, Cornelius, 10

Truscott, Francis Wyatt, 87

Tuck, David, 33

Tulloch, John, 24,25,38-40

Turner, J.M.W., 87

Turner, Richard, 32

Vailima, Samoa, 114

Victoria, Queen, 27,55,64,66,70,80,88,89,94,97,123

Visitors Guide to Bournemouth and its Neighbourhood, The, 23,25,27

Waddelow, Revd S.R., 40,70

Wallace, Alfred Russel, 75

Walton House, 64

Wanklyn, Revd S.R., 22,40,70

Weekes, Sir Henry, 49

Westbourne, 39,55,118,128

Westover Villas, 27,28

Wickens, John, 10

Wimborne, Lady Cornelia, 121,122

Winterborne Kingston, 14

Winton, 118,128,130

Woodhead, Felicity A., 12

Woodland, W Lloyd, 126

World War, First, 71,79,98,106,132

World War, Second, 71,92,114,122,136

Other titles published by The History Press

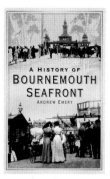

A History of Bournemouth Seafront

ANDREW EMERY

Published to celebrate the renovation of Boscombe pier, this is the definitive social history of Bournemouth from the nineteenth century when it was little more than a remote and barren heathland, its subsequent popularity as a spa resort in the Edwardian period, and its present status as a leading destination for family holidays.

978 0 7524 4717 9

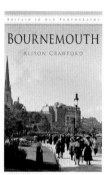

Bournemouth: In Old Photographs

ALISON CRAWFORD

Bournemouth in Old Photographs offers a wonderful insight into the development of the town, from its earliest fishing villages to the growth of seaside resorts and coastal spas, attracting visitors from the surrounding counties. Alison Crawford explores development of the city through her detailed captions and fascinating photographs. This book will charm anyone who knows the area well and those who are visiting for the first time

978 0 7524 4943 2

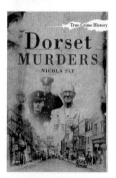

Dorset Murders

NICOLA SLY

Life in the largely rural county of Dorset has not always been idyllic, for over the years it has experienced numerous murders, some of which are little known outside the county borders, others that have shocked the nation. These include arguments between lovers with fatal consequences, family murders, child murders and mortal altercations at Dorset's notorious Portland Prison. Illustrated with fifty intriguing illustrations, *Dorset Murders* will appeal to anyone interested in the shady side of the county's history.

978 0 7509 5107 4

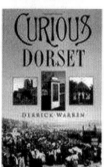

Curious Dorset

Derrick Warren

Dorset may well be the least spoilt county in England; a great many curious and unusual buildings, objects and landscape features have survived the centuries. This book is a guide to over eighty of these remarkable sights, together with some of the eccentric residents who have inhabited them.

978 0 7509 3733 7

Visit our website and discover thousands of other History Press books.

www.thehistorypress.co.uk